Elliot Richardson
The Virtue of Politics

November 2014

To The Ready Family —
With best wishes,
Tom Vance

Tom Vance

Foreword by Nicholas V. Prass

**IN MEMORY OF
DONALD A. CARR**

Environmental attorney, conservationist, avid birder,
and biographer of Elliot Richardson

DEDICATION IN THE 2000 EDITION

Kelly Elizabeth Vance, Andrew Christopher Vance,
John Daniel Boyle, Nanette Marie Boyle,
Nicholas Vincent Prass, Evan Wolfe Neu

CONTENTS

Author's Note
Foreword

AUTHOR'S NOTE

Works exclusively on Elliot Richardson appearing since the Council for Excellence in Government offered this as an online publication in 2000 include:

James Bennet, "Elliot Richardson: The Longest Day" in the annual edition of "The Lives They Lived," *The New York Times Magazine*, January 7, 2001.

Donald A. Carr, entries on Richardson in *The Scribner Encyclopedia of American Lives* (vol. 5: 1997-1999), edited by Kenneth T. Jackson, 2002; and *The Yale Biographical Dictionary of American Law*, edited by Roger K. Newman, 2009.

James P. Pfiffner, "Elliot L. Richardson: Exemplar of Integrity and Public Service," *Public Integrity*, Vol. 5, No. 3 (Summer 2003).

Tom Vance, "The Mentors of Elliot Richardson," *Massachusetts Historical Review*, Vol. 8, 2006.

Vivek Viswanathan, "Crafting the Law of the Sea: Elliot Richardson and the Search for Order on the Oceans (1977-1980)," Harvard thesis 2009.

Library of Congress *Finding Aid* to the Elliot L. Richardson Papers, prepared by Allan Teichroew and Brad E. Gernand, 2012, and revised and expanded by Karen Linn Femia, 2013.

FOREWORD

Who was Elliot Lee Richardson? Elliot Richardson was a statesman who put his country before his political party. He served in our government, most notably, as the Secretary of Health, Education, and Welfare, the Secretary of Defense, Attorney General, Ambassador to Great Britain, and the Secretary of Commerce. All of this is significant, in that it demonstrates his versatility in the political arena.

However, while these accomplishments are indeed impressive, I believe that Richardson's service in government is not his most important and enduring contribution. Rather, it is Richardson's unwavering fidelity to principle that stands out as an example for my generation, the so-called millennials. When he refused to comply with President Richard Nixon's order to fire Archibald Cox, the special prosecutor appointed to investigate the Watergate scandal, Richardson exemplified what it means to steadfastly stand on principle. In the end, he chose to resign rather than go against his conscience.

Too often in government today, our elected and appointed officials, both Republicans and Democrats, lack the courage and willpower to stand on principle, irrespective of the consequences they might face. Unfortunately, it seems that many of them would rather go along to get along instead of standing up for what they believe is right. Therefore, it is not surprising that many Americans have become cynical regarding politics and government. This is precisely the reason why I believe that consistent and principled politicians are what our government needs today more than ever. Perhaps this is the only remedy to curb cynicism among my generation.

Donald A. Carr, an attorney from Washington, D.C., who recently completed work on the first full-length biography of Richardson, passed away at the age of sixty-five in 2013. As this edition is being finalized, the status of his book remains unknown. I hope his great effort will be available to us soon.

~ **Nicholas V. Prass**

"[Richardson's] resume is enough reason for scholars of history and government to examine his life, if only to wonder how one individual managed to serve with distinction in so many roles."

~ Vivek Viswanathan, J.D.

Cover Photograph by
National Archives and Records Administration of
Ambassador Elliot Richardson during Law of the Sea negotiations

A grant from the Gerald R. Ford Presidential Foundation
assisted with research at the Gerald R. Ford Presidential Library
in Ann Arbor, Michigan.

1

SATURDAY NIGHT MASSACRE

"My God, he saved the Republic." ~ *Mary McGrory*

At 8:31 p.m., on Saturday, October 20, 1973, an urgent bulletin came across the United Press International wire service. President Richard M. Nixon had accepted Attorney General Elliot L. Richardson's resignation and had ordered the firing of the special Watergate prosecutor, Archibald Cox.

For months, Nixon had been consumed with the Watergate investigations. Both a Senate committee and the special prosecutor had been investigating the President's involvement in the cover-up of crimes by his staff and campaign workers during the previous year's election campaign. Burglars with White House connections had been arrested breaking into Democratic National Headquarters at the Watergate office and apartment complex in June 1972 in an attempt to gather political intelligence.

In the week before October 20, Nixon had urged Richardson to fire Cox, who was pressing for release of tape recordings the President had made of his Oval Office conversations, in some of which he discussed the Watergate incident. Richardson had disagreed with the President's demand, and they spent that week trying to negotiate a settlement. On October 19, Nixon sent Richardson written instructions limiting Cox's powers of investigation, and on the morning of the October 20, the Attorney General sent the President a lengthy letter outlining his position, along with last-minute suggestions for avoiding a crisis.

During his confirmation hearings for the post of Attorney General, five and a half months earlier, Richardson had promised the Senate Judiciary Committee that he would appoint a special prosecutor with broad powers to get to the bottom of the Watergate scandal. Richardson felt that he could not break this promise, and he told the President that firing Cox was not justified. In fact, the Attorney General was prepared to resign rather than

1

carry out the President's order.

On the afternoon of October 20, Nixon repeated his demand that Richardson fire the special prosecutor. The Attorney General stood fast. "I'm sorry that you insist on putting your personal obligations ahead of the public interest," Nixon said. "Mr. President," Richardson replied, "I can only say that I believe my resignation is in the public interest." There was nothing else to be said.

Because Richardson had refused to fire Cox, the President's order went to the next in command at the Justice Department, Deputy Attorney General William Ruckelshaus. Another public servant with a spotless reputation, Ruckelshaus had headed the FBI before becoming Richardson's deputy. Like Richardson, Ruckelshaus believed that the President's decision to fire Cox was wrong. He wrote a letter of resignation, but before it was delivered to the White House, the administration announced that Ruckelshaus had been fired for refusing to obey the President's order.

Finally, the third highest official in the Justice Department, Solicitor General Robert Bork, was ordered to fire the special prosecutor. He agreed to do this. Bork had also considered resigning, but Richardson and Ruckelshaus convinced him to stay in order to maintain some stability in the Justice Department. [1]

A CBS television newsman covering the late-breaking news from the White House lawn commented, "The news is coming too fast. Faster and harder than anyone expected. It is almost impossible to absorb." Three men who held top positions of public trust had been forced out that day. Where would it end?

The fact that Richardson had been such a loyal member of the administration made his resignation all the more shocking. Three million people from all parts of the country sent telegrams to Congress about the crisis, almost all of them supporting Richardson. The news media dubbed the resignation of Richardson and the firing of Ruckelshaus and Cox the "Saturday Night Massacre." In a special report that evening, NBC news anchor John Chancellor reported, "The country tonight is in the midst of what may be the most serious Constitutional crisis in its history."

Audio tapes were later released indicating that the president had, indeed, actively participated in the cover-up of Watergate from the beginning and had thwarted the FBI's investigation of the case. The House Judiciary Committee recommended impeachment on the following three charges: Obstruction of justice, abuse of Presidential powers, and trying to impede the impeachment process by defying committee subpoenas. With impeachment by the House inevitable and conviction by the Senate probable, President Richard Nixon stepped down on August 9, 1974, becoming the first United States President to resign from office.

The fallout from Watergate was monumental. Not only was a President driven from office for the first time in our history, but more than twenty of the President's staff and associates were indicted and convicted. Key White House staffers including the chief of staff were sent to prison. John Mitchell, Nixon's first Attorney General and the head of the President's 1972 reelection campaign, served nineteen months in jail. Richard Kleindienst, who served as Attorney General prior to Richardson, received a suspended one-month sentence. Maurice Stans, former Secretary of Commerce under Nixon and the finance chairman of the reelection committee, was fined $150,000.

Richardson's decision to resign as Attorney General rather than comply with the President's demand was the defining moment of his long career of public service and flowed from a lifetime commitment to the rule of law. Reflecting on Watergate, Richardson realized that the system had worked. Under the American system there is "a constant testing of strength among the three branches of government," he said. "The remarkable vitality of this process throughout all the years since 1787 would have delighted but not surprised the men who wrote the Constitution."

Twenty-five years after the Watergate break-in, the citizen watchdog group Common Cause organized a reunion of Elliot Richardson, Archibald Cox, and Sam Dash, who had served as chief counsel of the Senate Select Committee on Presidential Campaign Activities, which had investigated Watergate. During that June 17, 1997, ceremony, Ann McBride, the

3

President of Common Cause, recognized the contributions each man had made to the country in "one of its darkest hours." She stated the following:

> Far more important than the people who trampled on our Constitution and democratic form of government during Watergate were citizens like the ones who stand here today, Americans who successfully fought to preserve the rule of law. These three American heroes each helped prove that democracy works, that our Constitution can withstand the challenges of those who think they can violate the law because of their power and position.

While many American citizens became cynical about politics in the years following Watergate, Richardson continued to believe that, if pursued conscientiously, politics was the most difficult of the arts and the noblest of professions. His unwavering commitment to the rule of law and his dedication to public service make his career an outstanding example of the virtue to be found in politics. [2]

2

THE EARLY YEARS

"...Richardson would argue that nurture not just nature made him the man he became. [Donald] Carr reports that when asked to consider the importance of Milton Academy in his life, Richardson deemed only three things equal to the Milton Academy experience and influence: World War II, his work with Justice Felix Frankfurter and Judge Learned Hand, and his wife." ~ *Rod Skinner*

Elliot Lee Richardson was born on July 20, 1920, in Boston, Massachusetts. He came from a long line of physicians. There were three generations on his father's side and five on his mother's. Both families, descended from early New England settlers, had long traditions of Unitarianism, a Christian denomination stressing religious freedom, tolerance, and reason and rejecting rigid ideologies.

Elliot's father, Edward, was a surgeon and a professor at Harvard Medical School. The family lived in Brookline, a small town outside of Boston. The family's social and professional prominence probably contributed to the drive and self-assurance for which Elliot became known. A boyhood friend, who later became the editor of a foreign policy journal, observed that Elliot "carries into whatever he does the doctor's feeling that he's going to do the right thing." [1]

The family's wealth and prestige did not protect it from misfortune, however. Elliot's mother, Clara, died while giving birth to Elliot's brother George when Elliot was two-years-old and his brother Peirson was four. When Elliot was eleven, his father suffered a disabling stroke. Although left in middle age virtually unable to speak and with the use of only one hand, Dr. Richardson refused to give in to despair, and taught himself to paint and to fish. Dr. Richardson taught his sons "that truly worthwhile men and women do not impose themselves on others, that what counts is a private standard of achievement, dignified and quiet public service, not ostentation." [2]   The family attended the First Unitarian Church in Brookline, and Elliot would later recall that the central teaching at the church was respect for the individual.

Marguerite Brown, a social worker (and a Unitarian) hired by the family as a governess, helped to raise the boys. The household managed to maintain a "happy calm," one friend remembers, but Miss Brown (as the boys called her) also challenged them to high achievement both in school and in life. Intellectual success was not enough, she said. It was important to amount to something in life. She was a disciplinarian, but she was also notable for her open-mindedness. She was "an extraordinary woman," Elliot recalled years later, "whose strongest criticisms of other people were reserved for those whom she regarded as lacking in imagination. 'They travel around the world in a bushel basket,' she would say. And I took that to mean that they could not see beyond the confines of this basket." [3]

Henry Lee Shattuck (Uncle Harry) was another important influence on Elliot. An influential politician who served on the Boston City Council and in the Massachusetts House of Representatives, he taught Elliot that public roles were opportunities for service, not for pursuit of power. Elliot later explained that he patterned himself on his Uncle Harry. Shattuck taught the Richardson boys the art of politics and racial and ethnic tolerance. Uncle Harry endowed a chair in Irish studies at Harvard College during a period when many people scorned Irish immigrants. "He had no side," Elliot would say. "You don't hear that term anymore, but it conveyed a disinclination to distinguish among people on the basis of background, rank, or wealth." [4]

While his brothers pursued medicine, Elliot became interested in politics. At the age of eight, he was elected President of the Herbert Hoover Club at the Park School in Boston. He also developed a lifelong interest in painting and drawing. When he was in the sixth and seventh grades, Elliot was introduced to bird watching by Roger Tory Peterson. Peterson, a young art and natural history teacher at the Rivers School in Brookline, was then working on his first field guide to birds. Peterson taught Elliot and his

6

classmates how to draw and paint, "imparting to us his own enthusiasms for birds and other wild creatures," Elliot later recalled. "Roger Peterson was the only real teacher of drawing and painting I ever had. Starting me off with charcoal still lifes, he led me through the early stages of painting in oils to the year's climactic effort - a painting of a hooded merganser sitting on a dead limb in a forest pool. My model was a stuffed bird donated to the school by some unknown benefactor, and I wish I could say that the painting itself was as handsome as the bird." Peterson also tutored Elliot and his brother George when he visited the Richardsons' summer home on Cape Cod. As a young teenager, Elliot's ability to identify and draw birds was unmatched among his fellow students. He remained an expert on birds for the rest of his life. [5]

After retiring, Richardson wrote a tribute to Peterson in *Yankee*, a magazine featuring outstanding New Englanders. "Not only did he love the subjects he taught and take a personal interest in my schoolmates and me," Richardson wrote, "but he also rejoiced in enlarging our knowledge and arousing our curiosity."[6] Elliot wrote the following about Peterson's impact on his life in the foreword to the biography, *The World of Roger Tory Peterson:*

> I shall always be indebted to Roger for skills of eye, ear, and hand. Indeed, it may well be that through encouraging me to develop these skills he also gave me an even more precious asset: the ability to endure pressure and adapt to changes of circumstance. What could more quickly restore a sense of proportion than a few minutes spent watching a self-absorbed Carolina wren build a nest? What could more completely eclipse large concerns than the constraining effort to make hand and brush obey eye and brain?

Of Peterson's impact on society and the reach of his bird guides, Elliot wrote the following: "If we were to single out his most important contribution, would it be these remarkable books? His brilliantly life-like portraits of birds? His extraordinary effectiveness as a spokesperson for conservation and the environment? His greatest contribution, I believe, is the sum of these-our enlarged awareness." [7]

In 1933, at the age of thirteen, Elliot entered Milton Academy, a private prep school located outside Boston, which gave a larger scope to his

7

growing fascination with politics and public affairs. America was assuming its new role as an international leader, a role that had begun thirty years earlier, under President Theodore Roosevelt. As a boy, Elliot knew more about the diplomatic players in the League of Nations than about the baseball players in the National League. "By the time I got to high school," he later reflected, "I had come to regard the United States Senate's rejection of the League of Nations as a tragic mistake. In my eyes, Henry Cabot Lodge, the [Republican] Massachusetts Senator who masterminded the delaying tactics that led to this result, was a man without vision." [8]

Elliot's busy years at Milton would forecast his activities as an adult. He was involved with the science club, the student council, the bird club, the glee club, the student paper, and the debating society. He appeared in several theater productions, and was on a variety of Milton's athletic teams, including wrestling, football, and track. Academically, he earned an honorable mention and later a prize in Latin competitions. He belonged to the Cum Laude Society and received a Harvard Prize Scholarship during his senior year.

In 1937, Elliot entered Harvard College, joining his older brother, Peirson (George followed two years later). Elliot lived at Winthrop House and was active in many campus activities, including the Social Service Committee, the Undergraduate Athletic Council, the Nominating Committee (of which he was chairman), the Hasty Pudding Institute of 1770, the Signet Society (of which he was President), and the Class Day Committee. His athletic activities included the crew squad, wrestling team, and boxing. He also drew cartoons for the Harvard *Lampoon*. With a friend, he spent Wednesday afternoons at a senior citizens' home learning card games from the Old Men's Club, a group of elderly gentlemen who met once a week. Elliot enjoyed hearing them reminisce about their lives. "Although we felt we gave them very little, they were touchingly grateful for the mere fact that we were there," he recalled later. [9]

Elliot graduated Magna Cum Laude in 1941, with a Bachelor of Arts in philosophy. In response to the yearbook's question about career ambitions,

Elliot answered with one word: politics. "There, I was sure, lay the best possible avenue toward being of service in the cause of things I believed in," Elliot later wrote. One way to prepare for a career in politics was with a law degree. That autumn, he entered Harvard Law School, where he joined the boxing team. The six-foot-tall, one-hundred and sixty-five-pound student won the all-Harvard boxing title that year. He later called this "my greatest athletic achievement." [10]

Elliot's law studies were interrupted when the United States entered World War II. His poor vision threatened his plans to volunteer for the army. However, he memorized the eye chart, just as Harry Truman had done to enter the army during World War I, and did well enough to enlist as a medic. He went through basic training at Camp Pickett, Virginia, in the summer of 1942, and was nicknamed the "Harvard Man" by his tent mates. On request, he would entertain his fellow trainees by singing his favorite Louis Armstrong recording, "Bye and Bye."

Richardson was promoted to First Lieutenant during the war and was placed in charge of a litter-bearer platoon. Wearing red crosses on their helmets, his men had the job of getting wounded soldiers to medical care as quickly as possible. Assigned to the Twelfth Regimental Combat Team of the Fourth Infantry, known as the "Fighting Fourth," Elliot's unit trained in southern England to support the D-Day landing at Normandy, on the northern coast of France. On June 6, 1944, General Dwight Eisenhower, the supreme commander of the Allied forces in Europe, launched the largest amphibious assault the world had ever seen, the beginning of the Allied invasion to liberate France, and eventually the rest of Europe, from German occupation. A total of 150,000 troops and 1,500 tanks were ferried across the English Channel in thousands of ships while 12,000 planes supported Allied forces from the skies. Meanwhile, ships shelled the German defenses along the shoreline.

Eisenhower's troops landed at various beaches, with the "Fighting Fourth" storming Utah beach. Elliot and the rest of his medic detachment landed with the fourth wave. His baptism by fire came when his unit found a wounded soldier lying in a patch of barbed wire in a minefield. Acting fast, Lieutenant Richardson stepped over the barbed wire, picked up the

9

wounded man, and carefully retraced his steps out of the minefield. His medic unit saw intense combat throughout 1944 and early 1945. Elliot was wounded twice during the war and received the Purple Heart with oak leaf cluster. He also won the Bronze Star for heroism. His fellow soldiers nicknamed him "Lucky" because he survived his daring exploits. His unit was among the first American outfits to enter Paris when it was liberated from Nazi forces.

Throughout the war, Elliot carried a copy of *The Mind and Faith of Justice Holmes*, a compilation of the writings of the famous Supreme Court Justice Oliver Wendell Holmes (another native of Massachusetts). Elliot found Holmes's expressions of faith "deeply moving and even consoling," because he "spoke from the depths of his own Civil War experience." Like many people who have lived through combat, Elliot's experiences in World War II significantly influenced his life. He recalled later that those were "the most intense experiences of my life. I suppose the most powerful attitude it burned into me was a disposition to take one thing at a time and push aside fear. I thought I was going to be killed. The casualties were so heavy, it was just a given. I learned to take each day, each mission, as it came. That's an attitude I've carried into my professional life. I take each case, each job, as it comes." [11]

Returning from the war, Elliot resumed his law studies in 1945, at Harvard Law School, still convinced that it was the best preparation for a career in public service. During his first year, he made the "exciting discovery that thinking like a lawyer requires the ability to move quickly from the concrete to the abstract, from facts to principles, and back again without grinding gears…Though every legal task demands this skill, it is especially important in the effort to frame public policy in a way that is properly responsive to human needs and predicaments. The question is always: How will the general rule work in practice?" [12]

One of his professors was Archibald Cox, who would later play such a critical role during the Watergate scandal. "I well remember the impression he made," Elliot recalled later, "pacing up and down the platform with long deliberate strides, he looked like a great blue heron about to spear an unsuspecting minnow."

Elliot was struck by Cox's fairness, "one of the most conspicuous of many outstanding qualities." Elliot was tremendously impressed by the intellectual integrity of his professors. "Not that they preached," he recalled later. "The rigor of their analysis, rather, left no room for the false, the meretricious, or the self-serving. It framed the premises of their teaching: justice as fairness, the law's regard for human dignity, and the primacy of the public interest. In a long career, I have never felt the need for other precepts." [13]

Elliot served as editor of the *Harvard Law Review*, a top distinction, and he graduated with high honors in 1947. The new lawyer spent the next three years clerking for two of the country's most revered jurists, Learned Hand and Felix Frankfurter. Elliot moved to New York City to work for Judge Hand at the United States Court of Appeals during 1947, and the first half of 1948. The young clerk considered Judge Hand the closest thing to a great man he had yet encountered. "He immediately disarmed whatever uneasiness one might have had in dealing with this towering figure in the law by being down-to-Earth, friendly, and funny," Elliot recalled. As Hand's law clerk, Elliot's job was to be prepared to respond to any questions the judge might have about the cases he had heard. "The experience of learning how to get straight to the core of a problem proved to be of immense value later when I had a long succession of responsibilities in large, complex government departments." [14]

In July of 1948, Elliot moved to Washington, D.C., to work at the United States Supreme Court for Justice Felix Frankfurter. Frankfurter's other clerk at the time, William T. Coleman Jr., would later serve alongside Richardson in President Gerald Ford's Cabinet.

Justice Frankfurter gave Elliot advice that he would follow his entire life in managing his ever-changing occupational challenges. "I don't think you ought to develop career goals," Frankfurter told his young clerk. "I've known quite a few men who did this, and then they did everything in their power to fulfill this ambition. They were constantly calculating how to take advantage of some opportunity or connection that would move them along toward their goal. Yet, most of them awaken in their fifties to the realization that they are never going to achieve their great ambition. On top of that disappointment, they realize that they undercut the satisfaction of what they were doing by trying to use it for the sake of something else." [15]

In 1949, having completed his clerkships, Elliot was admitted to the Massachusetts Bar and then received a wonderful opportunity. He was offered the position of special assistant to the new secretary of state, Dean Acheson, in Washington. "I greatly admired Acheson and I felt torn between this tempting opportunity and the aim of learning the lawyer's trade," he said later. "The idea of being in the State Department was exciting. On the other hand, I always had in the back of my mind going into politics. If I stayed in Washington, I might end up a government hack." [16]

While wrestling with this decision, Elliot visited Harvard and happened to run into Professor Cox. Knowing that Cox had worked in government, the young man put his dilemma to his former professor and asked for advice. Cox replied, "Well, Elliot, when I was in Washington, I always thought it important to come from somewhere," meaning that it was important to arrive in Washington, D.C., with practical working experience and a solid reputation back home before tackling a bigger arena. Elliot decided to act on Cox's advice. He took a job working as a lawyer at Ropes and Gray, a reputable old Boston law firm. Elliot later looked back on Cox's counsel "with special gratitude," since gaining experience in a law practice in his home town "made a profound difference to my whole future." He commented, "I can't imagine what a different life I would have had, if I had stayed in Washington." [17]

One year later, Elliot became involved in politics at the grassroots level. He became a town meeting member of precinct ten in Brookline, serving as secretary of the committee dealing with the structure of town government.

In 1951, Elliot wrote a fifty-four-page article titled, "Freedom of Expression and the Function of the Courts," for the *Harvard Law Review*, the first of many important pieces he published during his career. The article discussed issues in free speech cases at every level of government.

"The great battles for free expression will be won, if they are won," he wrote, "not in the courts but in committee rooms and protest-meetings, by editorials and letters to Congress, and through the courage of citizens everywhere." [18]

Elliot married Anne Francis Hazard, a native of Providence, Rhode Island, upon her graduation from Radcliffe College in 1952. They met at a dance, where Elliot made a pest of himself by constantly cutting in, she later recalled. She put up with it because he was a superb dancer. Anne took a job as a teacher in Brookline, a prelude to her future work on the importance of reading. The Richardson's' first child, Henry, was born in 1956. Their second child, Nancy, was born in 1958, and their third, Michael, was born in 1961. [19]

Ropes and Gray was an excellent place for a young lawyer to begin. Elliot and other associates enjoyed working on important cases and solving clients' problems. At Ropes and Gray, practicing law was considered a calling, not just a job. Elliot also found time to be a lecturer at Harvard Law School. However, something was missing in Elliot's life. He felt that working in the private sector could not match the satisfaction of doing "a good job for the public." [20] As a result, in 1953, at age thirty-three, he became a legislative assistant to Senator Leverett Saltonstall, a Republican from Massachusetts. He wrote speeches and press releases for Saltonstall. He met Richard M. Nixon at this time, and was impressed by the young Vice President from California, who seemed to be a rising star in the Republican Party. Elliot worked for Saltonstall through the Senator's 1954 reelection and then returned to Ropes and Gray in Boston.

Back in Boston, Elliot remained active in Republican politics. In 1956, he wrote the speech nominating Richard Nixon for his second term as Vice President, delivered by Massachusetts Governor Christian Herter during the Republican National Convention. By the mid-1950s, with the proper education, wartime experience, prestigious clerkships, and a few years of experience in law and politics under his belt, Elliot was ready for the first of many high-level government jobs.

3

POLITICS AND LAW

"He considered himself a politician. He believed in elective office, not just appointed office. It was important for him intellectually and operationally to run for office, to serve in a direct sense." ~ Jonathan Moore

For someone who listed "politics" in his college yearbook as a career goal, things were moving forward well.

In 1957, at the beginning of President Dwight Eisenhower's second term, Richardson was appointed as an Assistant Secretary of the relatively new federal Department of Health, Education, and Welfare (HEW). He was responsible for drafting bills for submission to Congress.

Although Richardson was a Republican, his passion for public service transcended political parties. An admirer of Franklin D. Roosevelt, the four-term Democrat President who held office during his youth, Richardson disliked simple labels. Like many others who joined the Eisenhower Administration in 1957, Richardson came to Washington with high hopes of building a new political consensus based on the belief that government was responsible for protecting the individual against the harshest consequences of economic or financial misfortune.

"We were embarking on an important joint venture whose goal was nothing less than the creation of an exciting new blend of conservatism and compassion," Richardson later wrote. "Our philosophy began and, some people thought, ended with an utterance by Abraham Lincoln which we quoted at every opportunity." According to Lincoln, "The purpose of government is to do for people what they cannot do at all or do so well for themselves." [1]

When HEW secretary Marion B. Folsom was away from Washington, Richardson sometimes attended President Eisenhower's Cabinet meetings in his place. In 1958, Richardson served as acting Secretary of the Department of Health, Education, and Welfare for four months during Folsom's absence. Richardson admired his boss's leadership and described Folsom as an unassuming man who never raised his voice, always listened carefully to all sides, and always made sure that he had all the facts.

Elliot's job involved work on a variety of issues. An economic downturn brought a rise in unemployment, with many people exhausting their unemployment compensation benefits. Richardson was asked to draft legislation to provide federally-funded benefits for unemployed families. His plan was accepted without debate by the conservative Republican leadership, but the economy recovered before his bill could be submitted for Congressional approval.

Richardson believed that "the only remaining issues with respect to government responsibility toward general welfare were issues of how, not whether, to deal with a visible need." Accordingly, he played a major role in drafting the National Defense Education Act, a response to the Soviets' successful launches of the satellites Sputnik I and Sputnik II in 1957, which fed Americans' fears that the United States was falling behind the Soviet Union in scientific research and technology. This legislation, enacted in 1958, made funds available to upgrade educational programs in science, math, and foreign languages; it encouraged students, through improved guidance and testing services, to continue their education; it trained graduate students for work in higher education; and it designated funds to develop innovative graduate programs in international studies.

During his three years at HEW, Richardson also helped to develop legislation on social security, public health, juvenile delinquency, and a children's bureau. Other issues requiring his attention included medical education and research, health insurance, hospital construction, and preventive care. He spent much of his time defending HEW programs against budget planners from the White House and Congress who had other ideas for the $2.5 billion department budget.

At HEW, Richardson also handled tricky political issues with ethical implications. During his stint as Acting Secretary, the Food and Drug Administration (the FDA) needed additional office space in Atlanta,

15

Georgia. The lowest bid made to the General Services Administration (GSA), which oversees acquisition of office space for federal agencies, came from a building owner who happened to be a Republican State Representative in Georgia and the chairman of the state Republican organization. Because the building failed to meet the FDA's sanitation requirements, the GSA began looking elsewhere for competitive bids. Richardson immediately began receiving phone calls from senior administration officials and Georgia Republicans pressuring him to approve the questionable bid.

"It was also apparent that the career civil servants in HEW were watching closely, to see which way I moved and why," Richardson later recalled. He decided to support the GSA and resist political pressure to compromise the FDA's standards. [2]

During a reception at HEW for some Russian visitors, Richardson found himself speaking with the Soviet Embassy's cultural attaché. The guest said, "You know, we in the Soviet Union believe that the people exist to serve the state, while you in the United States believe that the state exists to serve the people. But aren't these, after all, merely different ways of saying the same thing?" Although Richardson guessed that the gentleman was just trying to make polite conversation, he could not allow the comment to go unanswered. "I'm afraid I can't agree," Richardson told the Russian diplomat. "For you, the state is an entity with purposes of its own that the people can be required to serve. For us the word is only a label for the arrangements by which we the people delegate to some among us responsibility for things that concern us in common." [3]

Having made his mark at HEW, in 1959, Richardson was offered a new job by President Eisenhower, United States Attorney for Massachusetts, and the family moved back to Boston. There he served as the top criminal law enforcement official in Massachusetts, representing the federal government. During his first few weeks in the new position, political 'friends' called to lobby him concerning pending cases. He told them that he would not entertain requests based on political patronage rather than legal merit. As a result, the number of calls declined as word spread that the new United

16

States Attorney would not compromise himself or his office. Richardson took pride in the fact that, during his tenure as United States attorney, every tax evader prosecuted by his office was convicted and sent to jail. [4]

The following year, in 1960, Senator John F. Kennedy defeated Vice President Richard Nixon in the Presidential Election. The new President appointed his brother, Robert F. Kennedy, as the new U.S. Attorney General. The position of United States Attorney for Massachusetts was a political appointment, serving at the will of the Attorney General at the time, and Robert Kennedy appointed a Democrat to replace Richardson. Elliot did spend part of 1961 as Special Assistant to the U.S. Attorney General wrapping up his duties as U.S. Attorney.

Richardson was disappointed by the Republican loss of the White House in 1960. He thought that a little more "modern Republicanism" could have spelled the difference between defeat and victory in the race between Richard Nixon and John Kennedy. The election had been decided by less than one vote per precinct. Richardson believed that the Republicans could have used the four years of Eisenhower's second term "to show that individualism could be both compassionate and creative." He believed that Nixon's defeat cleared the field for a less progressive brand of individualism, which would hurt the Republican Party. [5]

Richardson resumed his legal work as a partner at Ropes and Gray from 1961 to 1964. During this time, he unsuccessfully ran for state Attorney General in the 1962 Massachusetts Republican Primary. In 1964, a few weeks before the Republican State Convention, John Volpe, a candidate for Governor, asked Richardson to be his running mate. At first, Richardson was not interested because the traditional duties of Lieutenant Governor were largely ceremonial. He did not see the point in taking the job just to improve his chances for a higher position later. "But then it occurred to me that I might be able to make use of my experience in HEW," he later recalled. He told Volpe that he would run, but only if he were given responsibility for coordinating the state's health, education, and welfare programs. Volpe agreed. The two men were victorious in the fall election. [6]

Richardson's new duties in the Massachusetts statehouse included meeting regularly with the heads of the human resources agencies. This included public welfare, public health, mental health, vocational rehabilitation, education, corrections, and youth services. Although his department heads and he identified duplicated or missing services, these problems were difficult to solve. The system at the federal level encouraged fragmentation among state agencies instead of unifying them. Agencies would subdivide a person's situation and a number of agencies would attempt to help, each addressing only a small part of the total problem. "Not only are the agencies devoted to helping people too numerous, too limited in function, and too isolated from each other," Richardson wrote, "but they can be fiercely jealous in protecting their own turf. No wonder that government is so often perceived as impersonal and indifferent." Richardson decided that these state agencies needed to engage in joint planning and needed to be granted power to make the necessary changes.

Richardson helped to obtain a grant from HEW to improve coordination between volunteer and public state agencies. Richardson's legislative assistant and he drafted federal legislation called the Community Services Act of 1966, to provide incentives for state agencies that cooperated with one another. During his term as Lieutenant Governor, Richardson ran a successful statewide campaign to win passage of a sales tax to help the poorest cities in the state. He also headed the task force that initiated the state's Mental Health Act.

In 1966, Richardson again ran for the post of Attorney General of Massachusetts. His campaign focused on government responsiveness to citizens. He promised to create two new programs, a Citizens' Aid Bureau and a Consumer Protection Division. He won the election and, upon taking office in 1967, he immediately created a commission to conduct a complete assessment of law enforcement in the state. To strengthen the fight against organized crime, he prompted the state legislature to authorize court-ordered wiretapping by law enforcement agencies. He also worked for passage of a witness immunity bill, which passed in the House but failed in the Senate. In other areas, Elliot pushed through consumer protection laws and prosecuted consumer fraud and unfair trade practice cases.

18

Richardson addressed issues outside the state as well. As a member of the executive committee of the National Association of Attorneys General, Elliot worked for improvements in how money was distributed to the states by the U.S. Department of Justice. Richardson rounded up support for the change from Governors, Lieutenant Governors, and his fellow state Attorneys General. The reform was approved by Congress, giving states more flexibility and more control of monies coming from Washington. As a result of his efforts, allotted funds went to criminal justice planning commissions in each state, which determined how to allocate the funds, rather than going directly to specific projects.

Richardson also testified before a Congressional committee in favor of court-ordered wiretaps of individuals suspected of serious crimes. Ultimately, the Safe Streets Act was adopted, which "has since proved to be a valuable weapon against organized crime." [7]

By the age of forty-eight, Richardson had added to his experience as an attorney and Presidential appointee two highly visible statewide elected offices. He was about to return to Washington D.C., where he could apply his intellect and administrative abilities at a higher level.

4

FOGGY BOTTOM

"He was an extraordinary person, brilliant, able, honest, and liked by all."
~ *Summer Gage Whittier*

"...Richardson had been seriously discussed as a dark-horse candidate for the Republican nomination for the presidency in 1968; his stature may have influenced Nixon's decision to offer him the position at State when the new administration came into office." ~ *Geoffrey Kabaservice*

Richard Nixon's victory in the 1968 Presidential election was good news for Richardson. It provided new opportunities for Republicans to move into key Washington posts.

President-elect Nixon chose William P. Rogers as his Secretary of State. Rogers knew Richardson from the Eisenhower administration, in which Rogers had served as Attorney General and Richardson had served under him as United States Attorney for Massachusetts. They had worked well together and had remained friends.

A front-page story in *The New York Times* on December 31, 1968, carried the headline, "Rogers Picks Bostonian to Be His Chief Deputy." The job offered to Richardson was Under Secretary of State, the number two position at the State Department (comparable to Deputy Secretary of State today). The following week, Nixon and Rogers held a press conference at which they announced Richardson's acceptance of the appointment, along with acceptances by other senior appointees. Nixon said that Richardson's record "has demonstrated an immense capability as an administrator." As second-in-command at the State Department, Richardson would be responsible for administering the department, but his duties would also include policy matters. Rogers told reporters that Richardson would serve as his "alter ego." News accounts of the press conference, again making front pages as the Nixon administration took shape, described Richardson as an impressive public servant with a "zest for life."

Although the President appoints Cabinet officers and other key appointees, the Constitution requires that the United States Senate approve those nominations. Within two weeks, Richardson was testifying before the Senate Committee on Foreign Relations. His resume was impressive. Beyond his jobs in government and his law practice, Richardson was on the board of directors of the Massachusetts Bay United Fund, was a member of the Board of Overseers of Harvard University, and was Vice Chairman of the Visiting Committee of the John F. Kennedy School of Government at Harvard. He also served on the boards of trustees of the Brookline Public Library, the Cambridge Drama Festival, Radcliffe College, and Massachusetts General Hospital.

Senator Edward Brooke, a Republican from Massachusetts, introduced the nominee. "Elliot Richardson is an avid and understanding student of foreign affairs," he told the committee. "He brings to his new duties an inquiring mind, good judgment and, perhaps most important of all, fresh perspectives and a receptivity to new solutions for old and vexing problems." Richardson's former boss Leverett Saltonstall, by then retired from the Senate, submitted a letter to the committee assuring them that they would find the nominee "intelligent, articulate, and of sound judgment in the many difficult situations which he will face." [1]

Addressing the Senate Committee on Foreign Relations, Richardson explained his qualifications. He discussed how he had benefitted throughout his career from the men under whom he had worked. "I think it can fairly be said in each of these roles I have been a loyal lieutenant," he said. The Senate approved the appointment and Richardson was sworn into office on January 24, 1969, joining the State Department twenty years after he had turned down an opportunity to work there under Dean Acheson.

He quickly demonstrated his great appetite for work and his ability to master complex subjects. "He is the rare senior official who, presented with a one-thousand page report on one day, will return it the next, with underlining and commentary," wrote Christopher Lydon. He worked from 8 a.m. to 8 p.m., six days a week, reviewing piles of material in his dark

21

paneled office. The topics he followed included strategic weapons, the Vietnam War, and the Cold War tensions between the United States and the Soviet Union. His ability to absorb details rapidly, his administrative skills, and his willingness to listen and respond to the department's professionals made him popular. Career diplomats and staff at Foggy Bottom appreciated a newcomer who could articulate their issues and champion their department. The headquarters for the State Department received the nickname Foggy Bottom since it was located in a neighborhood that had been built on marshland in the early days of Washington, D.C. [2]

Richardson became the link between the State Department and the White House. Henry Kissinger, the National Security Adviser, was President Nixon's top foreign policy consultant. Richardson and Kissinger usually met at least once a week over lunch to discuss international issues. Richardson attended meetings of the National Security Council, a group composed of the President's top foreign policy and defense advisers. He also served as chairman of the Under Secretaries Committee, which included people like him who held second-in-command positions in Cabinet departments.

Within a month of assuming his duties, Richardson flew to Paris to represent the United States at a meeting with nineteen nations discussing economic cooperation and trade. In the fall of 1969, he delivered an important foreign policy speech for the Nixon administration in New York City. His message focused on the United States' use of military force to protect American allies around the world, and the administration's wish to prevent future entanglements such as Vietnam. The Under Secretary worked on developing Nixon's new China policy, which involved the lifting of trade and travel restrictions. He was active in negotiating limits for strategic weapons. He worked on European security issues and on increased efforts by the State Department to fight illegal drug trafficking. He encouraged the Organization of American States to intervene to resolve tensions between Honduras and El Salvador. He dealt with the seizure of United States tuna boats in international waters by countries attempting to extend their territorial limits. He coordinated delivery of food to starving people in Biafra, a province of Nigeria. He worked with Arab and Israeli ambassadors and realized then, ahead of many others, that there would never be peace in the Middle East until the Palestinians were involved in the negotiations on equal footing.

Meanwhile, the war in Vietnam raged on and the administration agonized over how to bring it successfully to a close. The United States strategy at the time, called Vietnamization, was to increase South Vietnam's ability to fight against North Vietnam on its own, allowing for the withdrawal of American troops. The Nixon team was also developing a "get tough" policy toward North Vietnam to try to force it to negotiate. Richardson publicly articulated this policy in a speech at the American Political Science Association's 1969 convention in New York City. "The large powers have found it increasingly difficult to determine the appropriate response to small-power provocation," he stated. "The strategic concept of a graduated response has been undermined by the Vietnam experience. If the large power voluntarily abstains from using its full power or feels the strategic situation to be such that it cannot do so, it in effect loses the advantage of being a big power."

In May of 1970, American and South Vietnamese troops attacked North Vietnamese forces operating staging areas inside Cambodia, which bordered South Vietnam. The administration argued that as long as United States soldiers were stationed in South Vietnam, the existence of these safe havens (called safe havens due to the fact that the United States was not at war with Cambodia) posed significant threats to American troops. Although the two-month mission was a military success, public reaction in the United States was extremely negative.

A delegation of fifteen of Richardson's friends and former Harvard classmates traveled to his office in Washington asking him to denounce the operation. Because Richardson had often been associated with the liberal or "Eastern Establishment" wing of the Republican Party, this group hoped that he would oppose what they saw as an invasion. The Under Secretary, however, said the maneuver made military sense and would shorten the war. He offered no apology to his visitors. [3]

23

Within the department, Richardson worked on improving the organization of the United States Foreign Service, including unifying various branches of the service such as the United States Information Agency, the Agency for International Development, and the Peace Corps.

After a year and a half as Under Secretary of State, Richardson was described by one journalist as a "tough-minded realist, immune to the administration's own propaganda, and probably the most effective administrator at Foggy Bottom in the last decade." According to the reporter, Richardson "has dazzled older hands with his ability to master not simply the conceptual problems of foreign affairs but the snarled lines of the State Department's internal management." [3]

When Richardson was appointed, some skeptics had doubted his ability to handle the job, citing his lack of foreign affairs experience. His performance as the State Department's top administrator for a year and a half allayed any reservations about his abilities. Meanwhile, rumors were circulating about an upcoming change in the Cabinet.

5

MR. SECRETARY

"I consider my two and a half years working with Elliot at HEW to be the equivalent of several PhDs in public administration." ~ Donald T. Bliss

"As always with Richardson, what he said was given force by how he said it. When he addressed a group of college and university presidents in one of his first HEW speeches, one president reportedly turned to another and remarked, You know, it took three hundred years of training in Boston to develop that style." ~ Geoffrey Kabaservice

Richard Nixon told his top staffers in May of 1970, that Richardson would make a great head of the Department of Health, Education, and Welfare (HEW).

It needed a great head because one-third of the federal budget went to HEW programs and, the department – which had not even existed twenty years earlier – had become a huge, overblown, and unwieldy bureaucracy. The President intended to move the Secretary of HEW at the time, Robert Finch, over to the White House to serve as his counselor. Richardson was a natural choice to take over, both because of his previous experience working in HEW during the Eisenhower administration, and because of his reputation for being able to manage difficult bureaucracies.

In June, Richardson found himself testifying at a confirmation hearing before the Senate Finance Committee. One Senator told the nominee that he doubted that anyone could ever know everything that was going on in HEW, much less efficiently run it. Richardson responded by characterizing himself as a man "who measures his satisfaction by the scale of the possible." He was easily confirmed for the post. [1]

The department at which Richardson now took the helm was not the same as the one where he had worked in the 1950s. HEW had become sprawling and unwieldy. The number of programs administered by the department had tripled since the Eisenhower days, with funds going to forty-thousand institutions and agencies throughout the country. "When someone asked me what it was like to come back to my old department after nearly twelve years in other jobs," Richardson recalled later, "I said it was like seeing an old friend who, since we last met, had grown very fat." Richardson found that fifty-four programs overlapped with other programs, either in HEW or in other federal departments, costing taxpayers almost $19 billion for duplicate programs. [2]

Richardson seemed to be the right man to put in charge of organizing, managing, and slimming down his "fat friend." An article in *The New York Times* quoted Adelberg Ames, a Boston physician and a friend of Richardson, on the new Secretary's approach. "He really believes that problems are amenable to analysis, and it doesn't really matter what the problem is as long as you have the technique for analyzing it." Richardson said, "I soon learned that the problem was not that HEW was unmanageable. Having served there before and having also spent two years dealing with health, education, and welfare problems in Massachusetts, I did not find it impossibly difficult to get on top of the day-to-day administration of the department. But tending machinery was one thing; defining what we were trying to do and why we were doing it, and developing ways to measure how well the job was done – this was something else again." [3]

Richardson distributed a memo to his managers titled, "Performance Priorities," in which he wrote, "my most important task must be an attempt to bring the monster under democratic direction and control." His priorities would be welfare reform, development of a multifaceted health care program, and the operational integration of human services.

According to the December 11, 1972 *Newsweek*, Richardson mastered HEW's programs "in short order" and instilled a new sense of purpose in its more than one-hundred thousand employees. The *National Journal* reported that he had developed a reputation on Capitol Hill as "a masterful witness, who could speak with authority on a wide range of subjects regardless of their complexity." [4]

In July of 1970, Richardson spoke in Atlanta at the annual meeting of the National Association of Counties. He said that he and his staff were filled with a sense of "excitement, urgency, and mission" in their determination to tackle the areas entrusted to HEW's care. Although he counted himself among the "chronic hopers of the world," he and his team realized their limitations. He knew it was easy to fall prey to the "Washington syndrome" of trying to solve social problems by simply throwing tax dollars at them and writing new legislation. He spoke of the need for reforms at the federal, state, and local levels.

Richardson dramatically improved the situation at HEW. He instituted a simpler grant procedure, consolidated programs, and promoted decentralization, in keeping with Nixon's "New Federalism," which made federal funding available at the state and local levels to allow more flexibility for local priorities. In 1972, Richardson inaugurated a national hypertension control program to lower death rates from stroke, kidney disease, and heart disease. For this accomplishment, he later received the 1978 Albert and Mary Lasker Foundation Award for Public Service.

Richardson also had many disappointments at HEW, as he would later recall. He was more supportive of busing to desegregate schools than was Nixon. The President insisted that HEW hold federally-imposed busing to the minimum required by the Civil Rights Act of 1964. The President vetoed a child care bill that Richardson had worked hard with Congress to enact. Elliot negotiated a welfare compromise with Democrat Senators, only to have the President reject it. Richardson's plan for health maintenance organizations also died at the White House level.

Despite the lack of support from the White House, Richardson "fought hard for the department's position," observed one reporter who analyzed Richardson's record at HEW. "Especially on busing and the cause of racial integration, on which he has a long and forthright history, he went back and back to the White House, trying to reverse the staff and finally the President." Richardson stuck to his principles even when he lost the fight. [5] He also lost the battle on passage of the Family Assistance Plan, which he later called "the most far-reaching welfare reform program ever put

27

forward." The program would have offered work incentives with extended benefits to low-income families. The House of Representatives passed this piece of legislation, but the Senate never brought it to a vote. It was later discovered that Nixon opposed the bill because of what he thought it would cost. [6]

Richardson's frustrations did not come exclusively from the Nixon administration. He knew that even a man with his managerial abilities could not succeed without significant reform of the department's structure. The *National Journal* reported that he told his staff that without Congressional approval for reorganization he could never rationally manage the existing structure. In 1972, he put forth a proposal for a "radical simplification of HEW's programs." His proposal, a two-hundred-page report titled, "Comprehensive HEW Simplification and Reform," called for a reduction in the department's programs from more than three-hundred to about ninety. The plan divided the remaining programs into three groups: financial assistance to individuals, financial assistance to state and local governments, and building the capacity of human services agencies. He always regretted that he left HEW before he could see the plan implemented. [7]

However, fate and history would call him to a task even larger than reforming HEW. In 1972, at the Republican National Convention in Miami, Richardson stood in for Attorney General Richard Kleindienst to discuss the Party's platform at a press conference. At the press conference, he was asked about the Watergate break-in of a month earlier. He answered the Watergate questions confidently, certain that neither the White House nor the Committee to Reelect the President (CREEP) could possibly be involved. "Quite apart from being both immoral and illegal, it was blatantly bush league," he later commented. Over the next year and a half, he would discover that his confidence in the White House and CREEP had been utterly misplaced.

FROM DEFENSE TO JUSTICE

"By breadth and strength of mind, he was very much his own man..."
~ John Thomas Smith II

In the 1972 Presidential Election, Richard Nixon overwhelmingly defeated George McGovern, despite emerging evidence that the Nixon administration might have been involved in the Watergate crimes. As Presidents often do when beginning a second term, Nixon reevaluated his Cabinet and announced several key changes.

Among these was Secretary of Defense Melvin Laird's return to private life. Richardson, who had now been at HEW for two and a half years, was the President's choice to head the Department of Defense. This meant that Elliot would move from the department with the largest budget to the department with the largest number of employees.

The President summoned his Cabinet members to the Presidential retreat at Camp David, Maryland, to break the news of the changes he had in mind. "On the helicopter ride up to Camp David, I had no idea what Nixon had in store for me," recalled Richardson. "At the outset of the meeting, I urged him to leave me at HEW because I felt that the work I was doing was important." Nixon refused, and Richardson felt that he had no choice but to accept the position at the Defense Department. [1]

Richardson's new post was announced in November of 1972, and the news was well received by Washington observers. The day after Nixon nominated Richardson for the position, November 29, 1972, David Broder reported in *The Washington Post*, "if the new Defense Chief seemed relaxed and soberly eager about his new responsibilities, it may have been because his whole career has been marked by frequent shifts of direction and a succession of diverse assignments – in each of which his performance has dazzled the professionals in that field."

Elliot again faced a Senate confirmation hearing, this time before the Armed Services Committee. Many of the committee's questions concerned the continuing war in Vietnam. When he began his first term, Nixon had promised to end the war. Now, four years later, Congress was under pressure to bring American soldiers home from a war that had become more unpopular the longer it lasted.

When the committee asked about the controversial so-called "Christmas Bombing," an air operation over North Vietnam that took place while Richardson was still HEW Secretary, the nominee said that this decision by the President was surely an "agonizing" one. He argued that the Commander-in-Chief had to do whatever he believed would reduce the loss of life over time. Asked if he favored the bombing, Richardson answered, "I think it would be more accurate to say I support it." Richardson told the committee that he believed this show of force was justified as a means of demonstrating to North Vietnam that the United States was serious about forcing a resumption of peace talks at that time. [2]

During the lengthy hearing, Richardson also answered questions about the defense budget, which many Congressmen thought should be slashed, since the war was slowly coming to an end. "Significant cuts in the defense budget now would seriously weaken the United States position in international negotiations," Richardson said, "in which United States military capabilities in both real and symbolic terms, are an important factor."

At the end of the three days of hearings, Texas Senator John G. Tower said that he had never seen anyone come before Senate confirmation hearings "better prepared to testify about the nature and responsibilities of a job that he has never held." Senator Tower told fellow committee members that he believed Richardson "is going to be one of the best, if not the best, Secretary of Defense we have ever had." The Senate confirmed Richardson's nomination on January 29, 1973, and he took office the following day. [3]

During Richardson's confirmation process, America's position in Vietnam changed. On January 15, Nixon announced a halt to all United States offensive action against North Vietnam as a prelude to a peace agreement that was signed in Paris, on January 27. These actions also signaled the end of the military draft which, like the war itself, had become more unpopular as time passed.

Once again, Secretary Richardson found himself wrapping up loose ends in one department to take the helm of another. Helping him in this task was Jonathan Moore, whom Richardson appointed to orchestrate his transition to the Pentagon. As a young man, Moore had been an aide first at the Defense Department and then at the State Department during the Kennedy and Johnson years. He then became a foreign policy advisor for Republican Presidential nominees George Romney and Nelson Rockefeller. Moore first worked for Richardson at the State Department and then moved with Richardson to HEW, where he became Richardson's Chief of Staff. He now served in the same capacity at the Pentagon.

As Secretary of Defense, Richardson's "greatest hope and firmest resolve" was to create a collaborative process that would fully engage the uniformed services in thinking through interrelated issues. These issues included the nation's responsibilities for maintaining a "stable structure" of international peace, the resulting demands on United States military capacity, and the various missions of the Army, Navy, Air Force, and Marines. Once these issues were resolved, he reasoned, other details such as levels of forces, training, and weapons requirements would fall into place. [4]

With American participation in the Vietnam War at an end, there was Congressional pressure to make significant cuts in the defense budget. Much of Richardson's time was spent reviewing and defending the $79 billion budget that he would officially present to Congress in April. He announced forty military base closings, including one in his own backyard, the Boston naval shipyard.

On April 10, Richardson presented the annual Defense Department report to the House Armed Services Committee. "Now for the first time in nearly a decade," he reported, "there is a realistic prospect that the United States may be freed from the travail of direct military engagement in Southeast Asia." After reading his twenty-eight-page report summary, he concluded,

31

"I am aware of the impact of the Vietnam War on public opinion and of the changes taking place in American society, events which have caused some people to depreciate the military establishment and to decry the need for a strong defense. I strongly believe that these people are mistaken." [5]

Years later, Richardson, along with other leaders, was asked to provide comments for a book, *What Should We Tell Our Children about Vietnam?*, Richardson emphasized that future students should understand that the United States "should never undertake a military action that cannot, whether for military or political reasons, be successfully carried out." Also, "because there are many situations like Vietnam and Nicaragua where decisive United States military action is not appropriate or feasible, the United States needs to exert effective leadership in pursuing alternative means of protecting its security interests through cooperative multilateral means." [6]

Although Richardson was serving in a high-level Cabinet position, Nixon conspicuously failed to reach out to him or to other Cabinet officers. Richardson attempted to initiate regular meetings with the President in order to get a "direct grasp of the President's thinking and add his own reflection to that thinking," according to the historian Theodore White. The two had one such meeting, which was cordial but not productive. The Defense Secretary wanted to discuss broad issues that shaped defense, but Nixon was not comfortable with such deliberation and responded merely with specific assignments for Richardson. From then on, the two met only for specific and immediate purposes. [7]

Richardson recalled later that, at first, Pentagon officials were "a little wary" when he took over, but, over time, they warmed up and began trusting him. "I listened. I understood what they were saying. I had a sense of what they had in mind," he recalled. "It was the same kind of approach that had served me well with the Foreign Service, at State, and at HEW." According to General Bruce Palmer Jr., who worked with him, Richardson had once again done a masterful job, accomplishing the most difficult task in supervising a new agency: the staff accepted him as a man of good faith, with similar objectives. "I liked especially his open-minded approach to the job and his willingness to try something different. Given the opportunity, he would have become one of our better Secretaries of Defense." [8]

As Richardson labored to master the workings of the Pentagon, the Watergate crisis continued to escalate almost one year after the break-in. John N. Mitchell, the Attorney General during Nixon's first term, was now accused of having authorized hush-money payments. There were media reports that the money had come from White House funds held by H. R. (Bob) Haldeman, the Chief of Staff. Richardson had been too busy at HEW and now at the Department of Defense, however, to pay much attention to the scandal.

Secretary Richardson took the morning off on April 28, 1973, to attend an event at the school his fifteen-year-old daughter, Nancy, attended. His visit was interrupted by an urgent phone call from his friend and former boss, Secretary of State Rogers. Rogers asked Elliot, "Are you sitting down?" He was calling on behalf of the President, he said. Would Richardson be willing to leave his new post at the Pentagon and take over the Department of Justice?

Richard Kleindienst had replaced John Mitchell as Attorney General when Mitchell became chairman of Nixon's Reelection Committee. Although not directly accused of Watergate crimes, Kleindienst was close to too many of those being investigated and was publicly blamed for allowing massive leaks from the Department of Justice. Mitchell himself was under investigation for his involvement in authorizing the Watergate break-in. The President had decided that Kleindienst should step down because it would be difficult for him to oversee the prosecution of colleagues. Meanwhile, the President had decided that he would ask his top two aides to resign as well. Chief of Staff Haldeman and Domestic Policy Advisor John Ehrlichman, both longtime Nixon friends, had been implicated in the scandal and their continued presence on the White House staff threatened to further undermine the administration.

A new Attorney General had to be appointed as soon as possible to restore public confidence, Rogers explained. The President and he had discussed candidates for the job, and both had agreed that Richardson was the man. Richardson, only three months into his position as Defense Secretary, was not anxious to make a move. He told Rogers that he would discuss the offer with his wife and get back to him with an answer.

"The prospect of having to take over the Watergate investigation was not pleasant," Elliot later recalled. Richardson and his wife Anne felt that he should avoid the assignment. At the same time, they realized that it would be difficult to refuse if the President insisted. Richardson contacted some old friends. They agreed that it would be better for the new Attorney General to be a fresh face in the administration. Richardson would be better off staying at the Department of Defense. However, they also understood why the President would want to immediately announce a replacement for Kleindienst. The search for an outsider willing to join the administration at this point in the scandal could take a long time. Richardson should push for someone else and see how the White House reacted. [9]

Richardson called Rogers back and recommended that an outsider be considered for the position. Rogers spoke with Nixon and called Richardson back within an hour. Elliot was still their choice. In fact, the President wanted to meet Richardson face-to-face at the Presidential retreat at Camp David the following day. Early Sunday morning, Richardson wrote notes to himself in preparation for his meeting with Nixon. The more he thought about it, the more he knew that he did not want the job. The attitude of the White House staff, treating this scandal with "arrogance, contempt, and a lack of real understanding," worried him even more than the crime itself. He concluded his notes with two unanswered questions. First, "what if the President did know about the cover-up?" Second, "do you have the stomach for it?"

Nixon started the meeting by telling Richardson that it was more important for him to join the Justice Department right now than to remain at the Department of Defense. The President told him that as Attorney General he would have full control of the Watergate investigation.

"Anybody who is guilty," said the President, "must be prosecuted, no matter who it hurts." The new Attorney General would decide whether to appoint a special prosecutor. Richardson would also remain a member of the President's National Security Council. Nixon then leaned forward and, looking at Richardson straight in his eyes, said that he had not known anything about White House involvement in Watergate until March, when he began his own investigation. "Above all, protect the Presidency – not the President if he's done anything wrong," said Nixon. He even told Richardson not to take the post if he thought that Nixon was guilty. [10]

These were the assurances Richardson needed to seriously consider the offer. He then gave the President some advice. "I hope you will respond to the crisis of confidence that Watergate has created by opening up your administration and reaching out to people in a more magnanimous spirit," he said, repeating a plea that he had made before, but to no avail.

Richardson remembers saying, "Mr. President, I believe your real problem is that you have somehow been unable to realize that you have won, not only won, but been reelected by a tremendous margin. You are the President of all the people of the United States. There is no 'they' out there; nobody trying to destroy you. Even the people who didn't vote for you want you to succeed." The President listened but did not respond. Richardson was now convinced of the President's sincerity in seeking the truth about Watergate. He was sure that Nixon had not been involved in the criminal wrongdoing. Although Anne still had reservations, Richardson decided to accept the post, concluding that he could be of real service to the President in this crisis. There really was not time to find an outsider. He would take the job for the sake of preserving and safeguarding the system. [11]

Following this decision, Richardson now wrestled with the need for a special prosecutor. Although he believed that he could meet the requirements of leading an independent investigation, he was concerned about public perception and public confidence in justice being served. He would be serving in his fourth key post in this administration. He was also aware of his own reputation for loyalty. "The struggle to preserve my independence would be painful," as he later put it.

At a press conference on May 7, 1973, one week after the announcement of his nomination to become Attorney General, Richardson told reporters that

35

he would appoint a special prosecutor if he was confirmed. Two days later, he faced the Senate Judiciary Committee. The hearings got off to a lighthearted beginning when the Committee chairman asked, "Did you ever hear of the Watergate affair?" After the laughter subsided, the seriousness of the proceedings quickly took hold. "All right," the chairman said, "Now, if you are Attorney General, what are you going to do about it?" The hearings lasted for three weeks.

As the hearings got underway, Richardson began collecting names of potential candidates to serve as special prosecutor. From an initial list of about two-hundred and fifty, he narrowed it down to seven. However, several of them were not interested in the position. Finding qualified individuals, prosecutors or trial lawyers of stature, willing to take on this untested post was proving more difficult than he had expected. One of his aides recalled Richardson saying, "It often seemed like we had become a nation where the only heroes were rock singers and ball players and that there were no large men of probity who could be called upon for the task." [12]

On May 16, 1973, Richardson placed a call to his old law professor Archibald Cox. Although Cox did not fit the criteria of being a prosecutor or trial lawyer, Richardson knew him to be completely above reproach and someone he could trust. Elliot began the conversation by wishing Cox a happy birthday, for he would turn sixty-one the next day. Although the two were by no means close friends, they had worked together as overseers at Harvard, and Richardson respected Cox's reputation as an individual of "unshakable integrity." Cox had served under Presidents Kennedy and Johnson as Solicitor General of the United States, responsible for representing the federal government in cases before the Supreme Court. He was widely regarded as one of the finest Solicitors General in history. Although Cox was a Democrat, Richardson did not see this as a problem for the administration. In fact, it would help to appoint someone without any clear Republican ties, and it would smooth Richardson's own Senate confirmation.

Over the next two days the two men traded phone calls, attempting to work out the details of the post of special prosecutor. Finally, on May 18, Cox accepted the position, subject to the approval of the Senate. Cox would report to Richardson and would be independent of the White House. Richardson would be the only one who could fire him. According to the guidelines developed by Cox and Richardson, the special prosecutor could be fired only for "extraordinary improprieties." Although the President publicly supported Richardson's selection of Cox, in private he began to worry that Cox and many others in Washington were out to get him.

Cox's biographer, Ken Gormley, noted that although Richardson and Cox led "parallel lives on opposite sides of the political fence," they moved in similar professional circles. Both were New Englanders who had successful careers in government and law. In fact, both had clerked for Learned Hand, where they learned a quasi-religious reverence for the law. Gormley wrote that both men shared precision of thought and expression, and both frowned upon all forms of exaggeration. "Trust in another person's word, even with no tangible assurance in writing, was mandatory," Gormley observed. That trust would be vital as the Watergate case became increasingly difficult. A newspaper report at the time stated, "The two men are very alike, self-confident, impatient of stupidity, exacting, publicly severe, perhaps snooty." [13]

According to Gormley, both men also shared a common vision of government, having first come to Washington when government was smaller and "basic codes of decency were assumed." During their early years of public service, government officials of high principle filled Cabinet posts and positions of importance in Washington.

On the penultimate day of the Judiciary Committee hearings, Senator Robert Byrd announced that he would vote to recommend Richardson for the post to the full Senate, but reluctantly, because the committee had not been given a chance to hold confirmation hearings on an outsider. "The Attorney General designate has been patient and cooperative, and he has conscientiously sought to allay every concern and every doubt harbored by Judiciary Committee members," Byrd said. He acknowledged that Richardson had selected an outside special prosecutor and had "revised, reworded, and refined" the guidelines governing that prosecutor in

37

response to committee members' concerns. [14]

Richardson was endorsed by the committee and approved by the Senate. Cox had Richardson's promise, and the support of the Senate Judiciary Committee, to have full and unquestioned authority to call any witnesses, review any documents, see any pieces of evidence, investigate any suspects, and prosecute any individuals involved in the Watergate crime. Richardson believed and hoped that the Watergate matter would be swiftly and fairly resolved.

7

MAKING THE SYSTEM WORK

"It was an ambiguous moment when Richardson acted – a time of doubt about the president's guilt, of concern that the scandal was undermining his authority abroad, of the seeming isolation of the special prosecutor – and it was his unambiguous action that gave the crisis some of the moral clarity we recall today."
~ James Bennet

"He provided a symbol of public virtue for society on the edge of cynicism. He helped turn a night when the FBI seized the office of the attorney general into a day when America's constitutional strength was reaffirmed." ~ Richard Darman

Part I
The Case Against the Vice President

Richardson was sworn in as Attorney General on May 26, 1973, in the East Room of the White House. Chief Justice Warren Burger administered the oath of office with the President, the Cabinet, and three-hundred guests in attendance. Richardson told the gathering, "This is a time when the institutions of our government are under stress...not because their structure is not sound. If there are flaws they are in ourselves, and our task therefore must be one not of redesign but of renewal and reaffirmation, especially of the standards in which all of us believe." Richardson told the gathering that the process of government had been infected with a kind of sleaziness that, as Attorney General, he would try to eliminate.

Richardson convinced key opinion makers that he was the right man for the job. *Time* magazine, for instance, wrote that "few men were better qualified by temperament and experience to serve as the country's chief legal officer." Indeed, he was the first Attorney General to have been both a United States attorney and a state Attorney General. [1]

The new Attorney General established the goal of strengthening public confidence in government in general and in the administration of justice in

39

particular. To do this, he needed to bolster the department's morale. In the Great Hall at the Justice Department, Richardson addressed department employees, reminding them of their department's objectives. "When I took the oath of office as Attorney General," he stated, "I said the first concern of the administration of justice must, of course, be the individual. The second concern is the truth. The first of these demands fairness, the second demands fearlessness. I shall do my utmost to be faithful to both."

Richardson conveyed the same message outside the department. Speaking in New Orleans at a meeting of the National Institute on Crime and Delinquency, he criticized the tendency of some people to view government as "them" instead of "us." He read the dedication from the book, *McSoreley's Wonderful Saloon*, by Joseph Mitchell. "This book is dedicated to the people who are sometimes called the Little People. Well, I want you to know they're just as big as you are, whoever you are." Richardson often quoted this dedication, he told the group, "because it expresses, better than anything else I know, my general attitude toward the responsibility of government." Justice in America must represent all the people, he argued, no matter who they are.

Richardson felt that federal leadership, through the Justice Department, could improve the administration of criminal justice at the state and local levels. One of his first acts was to ask his staff to research the prison system and investigate how to reduce the rate of repeat offenders. He felt encouraged, he later recalled, when he learned that the recidivism rate dropped when job opportunities were made available. He was looking forward to making this a top priority for the Justice Department. Richardson planned to link business leaders, community organizations, and the Bureau of Prisons to address the problem. [2]

Richardson brought with him the following three trusted aides: Jonathan Moore, J. T. Smith, and Richard Darman. Moore, who handled the transition from the Department of Defense, was Richardson's personal troubleshooter and associate Attorney General. Smith, Richardson's executive assistant, managed the Attorney General's schedule and helped him write speeches. Smith had been special assistant to the comptroller at

HEW under Richardson, and before that served in the Central Intelligence Agency as a program analyst in planning, programming, and budgeting. Like Richardson, Smith was a man of precise speech and thought. According to one Washington reporter, this made him an ideal first lieutenant. Richard Darman had served as Deputy Assistant Secretary at HEW, where he managed Richardson's staff. A Harvard graduate like Richardson, Darman had served as his special assistant at the Defense Department and had the same title now, coordinating top-level policy planning, management, and analysis. [3]

The new team was barely in place when crisis struck. On June 12, George Beall, the United States attorney for Maryland, visited Richardson to inform him about an investigation concerning possible corruption in Baltimore County, Maryland. Richardson smoked a pipe and doodled with a blue felt tip pen while occasionally taking notes. However, then Beall mentioned something that made Richardson pay special attention. Beall's office had been working on an investigation that could implicate Vice President Spiro T. Agnew. It was secondhand information, cautioned Beall, but he thought that the new Attorney General should be aware of it. Federal prosecutors had discovered that bribes and kickbacks may have been paid to state contractors during Agnew's years as a county executive and later as the Governor of Maryland. Richardson asked to be kept posted on Beall's findings.

On July 3, Richardson met again with Beall and three assistant United States attorneys from Baltimore, who laid out additional details of their case. The investigation had turned up incriminating evidence against Agnew. Richardson had two initial concerns. First, how would these accusations, if proven, affect the administration's ability to govern? Second, in light of the deepening Watergate crisis and its ramifications for the President, including the possibility that the President might resign, would it be possible for Agnew to assume the Presidency while under investigation?

The Attorney General asked his visitors for their opinions. What should the next step be? Should he confront the Vice President with this information? Should he inform President Nixon? By the end of the three-hour meeting, they had agreed that it was still too early to discuss the case with the

41

President and Vice President. With all the pressures facing Nixon because of Watergate, Richardson did not wish to needlessly worry the President.

Although the officials from Baltimore were impressed with the Attorney General's coolness in receiving such troubling news, Richardson was shaken by the revelations. From the very beginning, Richardson's solution to the case, if the charges were true, was for Agnew to resign. Richardson was in an awkward situation with respect to the Vice President, however. Both men were considered likely Republican candidates for President in 1976. There might be a perception, he worried, that personal motives fueled his interest in seeing Agnew resign. That evening, he told Anne that "a bad scene was developing" involving the Vice President. "It was a deeply disturbing picture," Richardson later admitted. "I felt sick, almost. It was as bleak a day as I'd ever had." [4]

The investigations of the President and of the Vice President continued throughout the summer and fall. Both investigations were ultimately Richardson's responsibility. The Watergate special prosecutor, Archibald Cox, was overstepping his powers, the President complained to his new White House Chief of Staff, Alexander Haig. Haig, a retired Army general, often discussed the matter with Richardson. Meanwhile, Agnew charged that he was being unfairly investigated, that he was innocent, and that he was being hounded by out-of-control young prosecutors in Baltimore.

By July 11, Beall's office had gathered enough evidence against the Vice President to warrant another meeting with the Attorney General. Richardson spoke at length on what they could expect from Agnew's lawyers, with whom Beall's staff had already been in contact. Richardson thought that Agnew would voluntarily resign if confronted with the evidence. The Maryland prosecutors, however, strongly disagreed.

One lingering issue was Richardson's possible conflict of interest with respect to the Agnew case. Should the Attorney General pass off the Agnew case to Cox, to add to his Watergate duties, so there would be no question of conflict of interest? Beall's team strongly opposed turning over the investigation to anyone else. Richardson felt that he could remain

42

objective. Beall argued that since the Attorney General wanted to restore public confidence in the Justice Department, having Richardson in charge of the case would be a plus for the department. Richardson finally agreed.

By July 23, the Maryland prosecutors had evidence that Agnew had also accepted payoffs after becoming Vice President. At a third meeting, on July 27, Beall's team reported to Richardson that although most of their case focused on payoffs to Agnew while he was Governor of Maryland, not Vice President, accepting bribes was a serious enough crime to warrant removal of the Vice President. They suspected that Agnew had probably told the President about his situation, and it was likely that the news media was on the verge of breaking the story. Richardson decided that it was time to officially notify the President and Vice President of the charges. He authorized the team to prepare a formal letter to Agnew advising him that he was under investigation for possible violation of federal criminal statutes. [5]

This step could not be taken lightly. Once Agnew was formally notified, the Vice President's reputation would be at stake and the burden of proof was on the Department of Justice. Richardson called Haig to request an appointment with the President. Richardson told the Chief of Staff, "They say, up in Baltimore, that they have enough evidence to charge the Vice President with forty felony counts for violation of federal statutes on bribery, tax evasion, and corruption." Agnew had discussed his problems with Haig, and had insisted on his innocence. Haig did not realize that the charges were this serious. Haig asked, "There's no mistake about this?" "There's no mistake," answered Richardson. "They've got him – the credible witnesses, documents, Heaven knows what else. In all my years as a prosecutor, I have never seen such an open-and-shut case." [6]

Haig knew that, coming from Richardson, this was a sobering statement. The general asked, "How soon before this goes public?" Richardson said that it was difficult to tell, since justice moved at its own deliberate pace. However, the investigation was almost complete. The next step would be to convene a grand jury. Hearing evidence and handing down indictments could take one month to six weeks. "At that point," Richardson noted wryly, "matters usually become quite noticeably public."

43

Richardson also explained his own predicament to Haig. "Richardson told me that he had subjected himself to a lot of soul-searching with regard to the Watergate scandal," Haig later recalled. Richardson told Haig, "I am trying to behave in a manner that when looked at six months to a year from now, will be good for the President." Haig said that he would arrange a meeting with the President. [7]

Richardson spent the weekend at his family's summer house at Eastham on Cape Cod, Massachusetts. On Sunday, Jonathan Moore stopped by to help Richardson plan his upcoming meeting with the President. Knowing that Haig always shared his information with Nixon, and that five days had passed since his meeting with Haig, Richardson released a formal letter to the Vice President's attorney on August 1, spelling out the charges. The letter mentioned extortion, conspiracy, bribery, and tax evasion. With this letter in hand, Agnew's lawyer officially notified his client that he was the first Vice President in American history to be formally placed under criminal investigation.

Richardson finally saw the President on August 6. The Attorney General summarized the evidence gathered by the United States attorney in Maryland. Richardson recalled later that Nixon seemed to receive the information in an objective manner. He appeared "disturbed and concerned with the correctness of any action or anything he did or did not do" on the Agnew case as President. Nixon said that he wanted another opinion on the case and asked that Henry Petersen, the Assistant Attorney General in charge of the criminal division, review the evidence. Petersen had worked his way up from a clerkship at the FBI to a career lawyer with the Justice Department, becoming the first career staffer to hold the senior Presidential appointment to head up the criminal division. Petersen had supervised the Watergate investigation prior to the appointment of Archibald Cox as special prosecutor. The Nixon White House had a high degree of confidence in Petersen, even though he was a registered Democrat. [8]

That same afternoon, at the President's urging (conveyed through Haig), Richardson went to the Vice President's office at the Old Executive Office Building. Reading from notes, Richardson summarized the status of the investigation for Agnew and his legal team. The Attorney General's summary included evidence that Agnew had received bribes while serving as Vice President, most recently in December of 1972. The Vice President interrupted Richardson. It was all a pack of lies, he charged. He did not trust Beall's office and he certainly did not believe the statements of the witnesses who were cooperating with the prosecutors, since many of them were also under investigation. Agnew wanted someone he could trust and, like Nixon, he suggested that Petersen head the investigation. Agnew's attorneys said that if ever there was a case for a special prosecutor, this was it. Richardson responded that although he had full confidence in Beall's office, Petersen could also take a look at the case.

Events now took place in rapid succession. The August 7, 1973, *Wall Street Journal* broke the story about the Vice President. The next day, Agnew held a press conference to declare his innocence. One week later, on August 15, Haig reported Henry Petersen's assessment to the President. Agnew indeed appeared to be guilty of the charges.

The President, consumed with the growing seriousness of his own crisis, wanted his Vice President to resign. With Agnew's departure only a matter of time, the President thought of his friend John Connally of Texas. "Stand by," Haig told the former Treasury Secretary. "You may be the next Vice President."

By the second week of September, Beall's team had informed Richardson that they believed there was proof that as much as $172,000 in improper payments had passed into Agnew's hands. At this point, it appeared that there was enough evidence to send Agnew to prison if the case went to trial. In an effort to avoid this unsightly blemish on the office of the Vice President, the Justice Department and Agnew's defense team negotiated. Richardson was ready to authorize Beall and his staff to present evidence to a federal grand jury if negotiations failed. The Vice President obviously wanted to avoid a jail sentence. Beall and Agnew's attorneys struggled with a plan to resolve the showdown and avoid a criminal trial.

The Attorney General personally wrestled with the dilemma of how to bring Agnew to justice. Any disposition short of a prison sentence would bring criticism that the Vice President was benefitting from his position.

45

Richardson later recalled, "The Vice President had a bargaining asset, however, that no ordinary person has: He was next in line to the Presidency. I saw no chance that he would resign first, then take his chances on trial, conviction, and jail." Therefore, Richardson kept looking for a solution. Haig later recalled that Richardson "wrestled with this question almost to the point of spiritual exhaustion; he kept telling me how tired he was as a result of his attempts to find a just solution." Agnew had committed serious crimes, Richardson told the White House Chief of Staff. "In the case of a Governor, we would recommend jail." [9]

Richardson contacted Haig on October 9. He could recommend that the Vice President not be tried or sent to jail if he resigned and acknowledged the evidence against him. Of course, there was no guarantee, explained the Attorney General, that the presiding judge would agree. Others at the Justice Department, however, wanted Agnew to serve time. "I must say it is kind of an uncomfortable position," Richardson told Haig. "I am going to make clear to my own people that this is the result of my own prayerful consideration." Richardson was concerned that everyone understands that he had arrived at this decision independently and that it was good law. "There is no question of that here," Haig reassured him. "There never has been." [10]

Vice President Agnew resigned on October 10, 1973, simultaneously pleading no contest to a single charge of income tax evasion before Judge Walter E. Hoffman in federal court in Baltimore. In return, the United States dropped all other charges and recommended leniency. Richardson appeared personally, representing the government. Considering the "historic magnitude of the penalties inherent in the Vice President's resignation from his high office and his acceptance of a judgment of conviction of a felony," Richardson recommended against any prison time. The judge declared from the bench that he would have sent Agnew to prison had Richardson not personally argued that leniency was justified. Hoffman sentenced Agnew to three years of unsupervised probation and fined him $10,000, reminding the Vice President that his plea was the "full equivalent of a plea of guilty."

A front-page article in the October 12, 1973 *Wall Street Journal* credited the Attorney General with resolving this governmental crisis. "Richardson is becoming one of the few major figures in either party who can command respect from broad segments of the public," wrote the reporter, Wayne Green. He noted that the serene and self-assured Attorney General had restored staff morale and public confidence in the Watergate-tarnished Justice Department in a mere six months. Green added that under Richardson's leadership the Justice Department had assumed a unique position of power and independence within the Nixon administration. Richardson was succeeding in his primary goal of convincing the public that the criminal justice system could effectively expose the shoddy side of government and the political process, Green wrote.

With Richardson at the Justice Department, politics was no longer a controlling force in the handling of major prosecutions and issues, a charge leveled at Richardson's two predecessors. One career lawyer at the Justice Department told *The Wall Street Journal*, "With Richardson at the helm, we've got a real Attorney General now – not some political hack."

Part II
Watergate

The summer of 1973 was a very long one for Richardson. He was caught in the middle of constant battles between Archibald Cox and Richard Nixon, over the authority delegated to the special prosecutor. Although the duties of Attorney General include acting as chief prosecutor for the government and serving as the President's legal advisor, Richardson could fill neither of these roles regarding Watergate-related issues. The Attorney General considered himself "attorney for the situation," meaning that all he could do was to cope as best he could with each problem as it arose.

The President constantly complained about Cox's handling of the investigation. Nixon later wrote in his memoirs that Richardson could not have made a worse choice for special prosecutor. However, even those closest to Richardson in the Attorney General's office, most of whom were Republicans, dismissed Nixon's complaints as White House paranoia. Richardson repeatedly assured the President that the special prosecutor was not out to get him. "Archie would rather cut off his right arm," the Attorney General told the President, "than take any action inconsistent with his duties." However, shortly after Agnew resigned, the President said to Richardson, "Now that we have disposed of that matter [Agnew], we can go ahead and get rid of Cox." Richardson later concluded that President Nixon had two goals regarding the special prosecutor. First, he wanted either to induce Cox to quit or to fire him. Second, he wanted his Attorney General to assist in that plan. [11]

Richardson lost favor with the White House over the summer because of the administration's perception that Cox had overstepped his mandate. Cox had subpoenaed eight tapes of Oval Office conversations that the White House had refused to surrender. More than once Richardson told Nixon that he should invite Archie Cox to "bring a truck over to Pennsylvania Avenue and haul away everything, including the tapes." If Cox found something, Richardson thought the President should just say, "Ah, shucks, I apologize, it must have been under the stress of work," and with that the matter would be settled. [12]

48

On October 12, a federal Court of Appeals upheld a lower court order that the President must turn over the tapes to Cox. Richardson was now walking a tightrope between the survival concerns of the White House and the enforcement demands of the criminal justice system. According to Watergate historian Stanley Kutler, the Attorney General realized the importance of finding a practical way of reconciling the competing interests of the President's desire for confidentiality and the special prosecutor's charter to uncover criminal evidence. As Kutler has noted, trying to this was a major focus of Richardson's role during the final three months of his tenure." [13]

Richardson was proud of his reputation as a team player. He wished to avoid a confrontation with the President. On October 15, Richardson met with Haig and White House counsel J. Fred Buzhardt at the White House. They informed Richardson that the President was willing to release an "authenticated" version of the subpoenaed tapes, but would fire Cox. The firing of the special prosecutor was unacceptable to Richardson. He would resign if the President fired Cox. During the daylong negotiations, a compromise called the Stennis Plan evolved. The White House proposed that a third party, an individual trusted by all concerned, verify the accuracy of the transcripts. The White House said that Senator John C. Stennis would fit the bill. A veteran of twenty-six years in the Senate and a former judge, this Mississippi Democrat would make a credible arbitrator. Richardson thought that this plan might break the deadlock, and he agreed to lay it out for Cox.

By October 18, however, Cox reluctantly informed the Attorney General that he could not agree to the Stennis Plan. The special prosecutor could not live with one person, selected by the White House, reviewing the tapes and comparing them to edited transcripts. Not only would this be a daunting job for any individual, but summaries of the tapes would not even be admissible as evidence in a court of law. On top of this, the White House was insisting that Cox not be permitted to subpoena any further documents. Richardson agreed that such future restrictions on Cox were unacceptable. "Slowly, but surely," noted Kutler, "events put Richardson in an untenable position." [14]

On Friday, October 19, Richardson went to work prepared to resign if necessary. "I called Haig and asked to see the President, knowing what I had to do." Instead, he met with the Chief of Staff. Haig, speaking on behalf of the President, tried to persuade the Attorney General to agree to have tapes that were verified by Stennis submitted to a court. The court would be told that this was as far as the White House would go, argued Haig, so Cox would not have to be fired.

Richardson was not convinced and was still at work in his office at 7 p.m. when Haig called to say that a letter from the President was on its way to the Justice Department. "I was angry and upset," recalled Richardson. The letter arrived twenty minutes later, in which the President apologized for his "limited" intrusion on his Attorney General's independence, but made it clear that Cox's future as special prosecutor depended on his accepting the Stennis Plan and making no further attempts to subpoena Presidential materials. The Attorney General called Cox to inform him of the letter. Richardson went home that evening and discussed this development with Anne. "It was clear that I could not carry out the instructions," he recalled. His predicament reminded Richardson of his experience as a medic at Normandy, making his way through the minefield carrying a wounded soldier. [15]

On October 20, the headlines in *The New York Times* read, "Nixon to Keep Tapes Despite Ruling; Will Give Own Summary; Cox Defiant." Cox called a press conference for 1 p.m. at the National Press Club in Washington.

That Saturday morning, Richardson worked on summarizing his notes of the night before under the title, "Summary of Reasons Why I Must Resign." He would use this as the basis for a letter to the President. Richardson then made the drive one last time as Attorney General from his home to the Justice Department to meet with his staff.

Richardson's letter to the President repeated the importance of the special prosecutor's independence, but offered several new compromises that would allow Cox to carry out his duties. Richardson's letter was delivered to the White House just seconds before Cox went on television.

50

The special prosecutor said that he would not accept the Stennis Plan and firmly stated that he would not resign. Later, in the foreword to Ken Gormley's biography of Cox, Richardson wrote, "In the end, Nixon's most damaging misjudgment was his underestimation of Cox's ability to communicate the strength of his integrity. Nixon, himself, like everyone else who watched Cox's press conference on the afternoon of October 20, 1973, must have felt that force. Indeed, in all the annals of public service there have been few finer examples of grace under pressure." During the question and answer period after he read his prepared statement, Cox was asked about Richardson's handling of the case. Cox replied that Richardson had acted honorably throughout the affair. [16]

The Attorney General and his top advisers watched the press conference from Richardson's sitting room at the Justice Department. "I did not have to wait long for Haig's call telling me that the President wanted me to fire Cox," Richardson later recounted. The Attorney General asked, "Al, when can I see the President?" There was no doubt in Richardson's mind now. It was a clear-cut decision. According to the ground rules he had established during his Senate confirmation hearing, he could fire Cox only for impropriety. There was no impropriety of any sort here. Haig invited Richardson to come over to the White House, where they spoke about Richardson's future in the administration. [17]

The two men stood together uncomfortably at a Constitutional crossroads, according to Gormley. "He talked about how highly the President regarded me," recalled Richardson. Haig even mentioned the prospect of a spot on the national ticket for Richardson after Nixon's present term expired. "Al, there's no way I can move forward with firing Cox," Richardson replied. Haig offered another proposal. Richardson could resign if he felt he had to, but not make it public for one week. Richardson dismissed the proposal and told Haig that it was time to see the President. [18]

Richardson entered the Oval Office at 4 p.m. and noticed that Nixon "seemed under more strain than I had seen him in previous years." Nixon started talking about the crisis in the Middle East, specifically the Yom Kippur War. And the Watergate case was hurting the United States position on an international level, the President argued – the Soviets will see this as a sign of weakness. Richardson had considered this during his deliberations the night before. "If it is that important, then don't push to fire Cox," Richardson later recalled thinking. Nixon then mentioned the same idea proposed by General Haig. Go ahead and resign, if you must, Nixon suggested, but sit on it for a while. [19]

Richardson shook his head, reminding the President that he could fire Cox only for extraordinary impropriety. Nixon said, "I'm sorry, Elliot, that you choose to put your purely personal obligations ahead of the national interest." In one account of the conversation, the Attorney General responded, "Mr. President, I can only say that I believe my resignation is in the public interest." Another account has Richardson saying, "Mr. President, it would seem we have differing views of the national interest." The historic meeting came to an end. [20]

Back in his office at the Justice Department, Richardson wrote a letter of resignation addressed to President Nixon that read, in part:

> At the time you appointed me, you gave me the authority to name a special prosecutor if I should consider it appropriate. A few days before my confirmation hearing began, I announced that I would, if confirmed, "appoint a special prosecutor and give him all the independence, authority, and staff support needed to carry out the tasks entrusted to him." I added, "Although he will be in the Department of Justice and report to me – and only to me – he will be aware that his ultimate accountability is to the American people . . . While the special prosecutor can be removed from office for 'extraordinary improprieties,'" I also pledged that "the attorney general will not countermand or interfere with the special prosecutor's decisions or actions." While I fully respect the reasons that have led you to conclude that the special prosecutor must be discharged, I trust that you understand that I could not in the light of these firm and repeated commitments carry out your direction that this be done. In the circumstances, therefore, I feel that I have no choice but to resign. [21]

After accepting Richardson's resignation, the President ordered Deputy Attorney General William Ruckelshaus to fire Cox. Ruckelshaus refused and also resigned, although the White House ordered his dismissal before his letter of resignation was received. The next in line, Solicitor General Robert Bork, planned to fire Cox and then resign. Richardson and Ruckelshaus convinced Bork to remain to "mind the store" and ensure continuity at the Justice Department. Some historians believe that if Bork had also resigned rather than carrying out the Presidential order, it might have hastened the end of the Watergate scandal. But Richardson and Ruckelshaus were convinced that it would do less damage to the Justice Department if Bork carried out Nixon's order and remained. That way, the Department would not be crippled during the time it might take for Nixon to find someone else to carry out his order. Bork, who supported the President's position that Cox had overstepped his mandate, signed a hastily drafted letter dismissing him as special prosecutor. This chain of events came to be known as the "Saturday Night Massacre." [22]

Before the day was done, Richardson called Cox to let him know the sequence of events regarding his dismissal. At the end of the conversation, Richardson recited a passage from Homer's *Iliad*, which Learned Hand had inscribed on a photo that he had presented to Richardson. "Now, though numberless fates of death beset us which no mortal can escape or avoid, let us go forward together, and either we shall give honor to one another or another to us." [23]

The following October 21 headline in *The New York Times* spanned the top of the page. "Nixon Discharges Cox for Defiance; Abolishes Watergate Task Force; Richardson and Ruckelshaus Out." The nation responded with shock and outrage. The resignation of Richardson and his deputy, along with Nixon's order to abolish the office of the special prosecutor, resulted in a firestorm of public talk of impeachment of the President. Letters and telegrams expressing outrage at the President's actions flooded Washington. *The New York Times* editorial on October 21, referred to Richardson's resignation in protest as "courageous." The next day, *The New York Times* editorial lamented, "this espousal of absolute rule has thrown the country into a governmental crisis of fearful dimensions." An October 23 editorial in *The New York Times* declared that "Mr. Nixon has brought the nation to

53

its most severe crisis since the Reconstruction era, when one President [Andrew Johnson] stood trial for impeachment and another [Rutherford B. Hayes] took office after the disputed election of 1876."

On Monday afternoon, October 22, Richardson met with Nixon for thirty minutes. The President wanted to know how Richardson was going to handle his public statements about the resignation. Richardson reassured Nixon that there would be no personal attacks. This was the last meeting between the two men. Richardson gave a public explanation of his actions the next day. With the permission of Acting Attorney General Bork, Richardson held a live, televised press conference in front of hundreds of Department employees at the Great Hall of the Justice Department.

The journalist Elizabeth Drew gave this report on the scene.

> As Richardson and his wife, together with Ruckelshaus, step through the blue velvet curtain, the Justice Department workers burst into prolonged applause. It is the sort of emotional applause that, once started, feeds on itself – the applauders' way of making a statement. The ovation also expresses the Justice Department workers' desire for a hero – a moral standard to which they can repair. An Associated Press reporter estimated that the applause continued for nearly two minutes.

Drew observed that the former Attorney General looked different than he had on previous occasions. "He is tired; his eyes are bleary. His voice is tremulous. His delivery lacks the customary crispness. He is apparently struggling for control of his emotions; it seems to be the fatigue, a reaction to the ovation the Justice Department workers have given him and to what he has been through," [24]

In a prepared statement, Richardson told his former co-workers and the television audience that, "At stake, in the final analysis, is the very integrity of the governmental processes I came to the Department of Justice to help restore." He did not dispute the President's authority to change the rules of the game, but he explained why he could not abide by that change.

54

Although he praised the Nixon administration's general goals and priorities, Richardson said, "I have been compelled to conclude that I could better serve my country by resigning my public office than by continuing in it." In response to White House plans to continue the Watergate investigations from within the Justice Department, Richardson and Ruckelshaus stated that a new special prosecutor, independent of the Nixon administration, was necessary to properly pursue the investigation.

An opinion piece titled, "The Constitutional Crisis," by the President of the American Bar Association, Chesterfield H. Smith, ran in the October 23 edition of *The New York Times*. It applauded the actions of Richardson, Ruckelshaus, and Cox. Smith wrote that the three "have emphasized to the nation that they are lawyers who honor the tradition of the legal profession and that they are lawyers who properly and without hesitation put ethics and professional honor above public office."

The cover of the October 29, 1973 *Time* magazine showed pictures of Richard Nixon and Archibald Cox with a split between them. The cover story was titled, "Richard Nixon Stumbles to the Brink," and included the sidebar story titled, "The Three Men of High Principle," referring to Cox, Richardson, and Ruckelshaus. Although Richardson was regarded as an administration loyalist, "his chief allegiance throughout his career has been to law," stated the article. The article also quoted Richardson as saying, "Law is the indispensable attribute of an ordered society." The immediate result was that Congress passed a series of reforms, including a provision for the creation of special prosecutors, so that the Saturday Night Massacre would not occur again.

In a 1990 poll, historians rated Watergate the greatest abuse of power in United States history by a wide margin. Richardson appeared on June 17, 1997, at a press conference commemorating the twenty-fifth anniversary of Watergate, hosted by Common Cause, an advocacy group for campaign finance reform and ethics laws. Richardson said, "This anniversary serves to help remind the American people that, in the wake of one of the greatest political scandals and misuse of power in our history as a nation, scandal produced important reforms that served this nation well for two decades." Richardson explained that the lessons of Watergate continue to be important because of the lack of public trust in government and politics. "People have moved beyond apathy, beyond skepticism into deep cynicism," he said. Citing the decline in voter participation, the 1996 elections saw the lowest turnout in more than seventy years, Richardson worried that people "are convinced that nothing can be done to make their voices heard in Washington." He noted that about $250 million in private contributions had fueled the campaigns in 1996.

Richardson said that the reform in Presidential campaign financing enacted into law in 1974:

> . . . worked very well for a long time and had strong bipartisan support . . . But now it clearly needs to be reformed again. This is true, of course, for almost any legislation: It will work well for a time and then need to be revised. The Watergate reforms did work well for many years, and if improved and broadened, these reforms can have real and major impact on the system today. Making those improvements will again require the bipartisan approach used two decades ago.

In an oral history for the Ford Presidential Library, Richardson reflected that someday he would have to write about the contrast between the Nixon who was a committed public servant, and the Nixon who was divisive, cynical, and vindictive. The contrast is wider than most people think, Richardson commented. When Oliver Stone and Anthony Hopkins paid a visit to the retired Elliot Richardson for their movie about Nixon, Richardson recalled that he "tried to get across to them the classic dimensions of the Nixon tragedy," which you cannot communicate unless you also understand the scale of the positive capabilities, ideas, and strategic capacity of Richard Nixon. [25]

Ruckelshaus later reflected that Richardson, as Attorney General, had been "subjected to the most intense political pressure imaginable" and that "the choices he made in a time of national crisis are a tribute to him and the enduring values of America." [26]

8

THE COURT OF ST. JAMES

"... [Gerald R. Ford] respected Richardson and was appalled by the Saturday Night Massacre. Restoring Elliot to a responsible post was a key part of healing the Watergate wounds." ~ Robert Trowbridge Hartman

"He was genteel in manner and might have seemed aloof, but not to those who actually dealt with him in person. For his personal interactions with people faithfully reflected his philosophical convictions; he was unfailingly gracious and courteous to others regardless of their status. At the personal level, there always seemed to be a twinkle in Richardson's eye, and his subtle sense of humor always lingered just below the surface." ~ James P. Pffifner

Secret Service agents had been guarding Carl Albert, the Speaker of the House of Representatives, since the resignation of Vice President Spiro Agnew. Albert was the next in line for the Presidency in the absence of a sitting Vice President. Agnew resigned in October, and it took until December to swear in a new Vice President.

The Twenty-Fifth Amendment to the Constitution, never before used, allowed the President to appoint a new Vice President in the event of death or resignation. When Agnew left office, Richard Nixon had the following five candidates in mind: Elliot Richardson, former Treasury Secretary John Connally, former California Governor Ronald Reagan, New York Governor Nelson Rockefeller, and Michigan Congressman and House Minority Leader Gerald R. Ford. Because of his role in Agnew's prosecution, Richardson asked the President to take his name off the list.

On October 12, 1973, two days after Agnew left office, Nixon asked Gerald Ford to take the Vice Presidency. Because the President wanted Connally to run for the Presidency at the end of Nixon's second term, he secured Ford's agreement to support Connally in 1976. Ford, a twenty-five-year veteran of Congress, was already planning to retire in 1977. He was confirmed by both Houses of Congress, and in December, he was sworn in as Nixon's Vice President.

Meanwhile, Richardson had adapted to life in the private sector. He was now studying state and local governments as a scholar at the Woodrow Wilson Center for International Scholars in Washington, D.C., a part of the Smithsonian Institution. He started work on his first book and went on nationwide speaking tours. The Watergate scandal continued to grow, and Richardson's principled resignation earned him national folk hero status. He was considered a likely Presidential candidate for 1976 should Ford decide against running.

Richardson made two-hundred and sixty speeches during his tenure at the Wilson Center, mostly to college audiences, civic groups, and Republican gatherings. He also lectured at the Lyndon Johnson School of Politics at the University of Texas, held a Chubb Fellowship at Yale, and was a part of the Godkin lectures at Harvard.

One of his addresses, "Vulnerability and Vigilance," was included in a series of great speeches, *Representative American Speeches*. These remarks were made at the Appeal of Conscience Foundation dinner in New York City, on December 11, 1973, at the Hotel Pierre. Richardson, introduced by Rockefeller, spoke before a crowd of five-hundred diplomats, politicians, and religious leaders. They gathered to support the foundation's efforts on behalf of religious freedom throughout the world. In his speech, later praised as remarkable for its restraint, Richardson called for protection against invasion of privacy, prevention of campaign abuses, erection of barriers against improper use of political influence, and enactment of provisions for stricter accountability in the exercise of power.

A front-page story in the February 22, 1974 *Wall Street Journal* noted that Richardson's speeches made the classic Republican argument for limiting the increasingly pervasive and, according to some, intrusive federal government. He also argued that whatever had been wrong in Watergate was not chargeable to the Republican Party, for tarring the party with the

58

brush of Watergate would be a flagrant case of guilt by association. Richardson was "coolly judicious" in discussing Nixon, the *Wall Street Journal* reported. He advised audiences to suspend judgment on the impeachment issue until the investigations were complete. Richardson said that he opposed demands for Nixon's resignation because resignation would leave a "residue of bitterness" with the American people. The former Attorney General did, however, criticize the President's continuing refusal to disclose all Watergate-related tape recordings and documents. The newspaper reported that Richardson believed that Nixon had to shoulder the blame for the combative attitudes within the White House that had led to the Watergate abuses. He would not have supported Nixon for reelection in 1972, had he known then what he now knew, he concluded. [1]

On April 28, 1974, Richardson appeared on *Meet the Press* and answered numerous questions about his views of the continuing Watergate crisis. Based on his travels throughout the country, he was asked if he thought that most Americans perceived the political system as corrupt and politicians as crooks. Richardson responded by saying, "I certainly do, yes. In fact, I think that the most critical danger we face right now is the danger that cynicism will bite so deeply that we can't effectively have a system of free representative self-government any more, and that is why I see the need now for a greater degree of emphasis on openness and candor in government than ever before in our history." Like many times before, Richardson was asked about his interest in the Presidency and what he would most like to accomplish as President:

> The key problems, at least as I see them today, involve, in the first instance, the further pursuit of a more stable world order. They involve problems of the domestic economy – inflation, energy – and they involve the kinds of things I am writing about, which have to do with the relationship of the citizen to government and the very possibility, given the complexity of our society, of preserving a system of free self-government. I think that, in turn, means that we can and should move in a direction that emphasizes the rebuilding of community and greater reliance on governmental units that are subject to the voice of the individual and to effective control by community people.

Meanwhile, the Watergate scandal had escalated to become a Constitutional crisis. Secretary of State Kissinger advised Nixon to resign. Even the ten Republicans on the House Judiciary Committee voted in favor of impeachment and condemned Nixon's conduct during the Watergate cover-up. Republican National Committee chairman George H. W. Bush wrote to the President to urge him to resign. Senate leaders meeting with Nixon told him that his support in the Senate had vanished. With charges leading directly to President Nixon himself, and with impeachment and conviction nearly a certainty, Nixon resigned from office on August 9, 1974, the only President in American history to do so.

Ten years later, reflecting on these events for a volume about the Nixon years, Richardson stated that Watergate had demonstrated the "strength and resilience" of the American Constitutional structure. "The checks and balances worked in an absolutely textbook fashion in that situation," he reflected. Later, in the foreword to a book on Watergate, Richardson referred to Archibald Cox's press conference the day he was fired as special prosecutor. Cox had said, "Whether ours shall continue a government of laws and not of men is now for Congress to decide and, ultimately, the American people." Richardson wrote in his foreword, "Professor Cox was right, with a difference. It was the American people who decided, and the Congress which concurred, that ours would continue a government of laws and not of men. The American people could not have made plainer their determination to maintain a government of laws," he concluded, citing the national public protest following the Saturday Night Massacre. [2]

Ford was sworn into office as President. His first important task was to use his powers under the Twenty-Fifth Amendment to appoint a Vice President. He solicited names of candidates from his staff and Republican leaders. Richardson was on the short list of candidates along with George H.W. Bush, Nelson Rockefeller, Barry Goldwater, and Ronald Reagan.

On August 11, Presidential assistant Bryce Harlow gave Ford an analysis of the sixteen leading contenders, with each man receiving scores for various traits. Richardson received perfect scores in the areas of experience, clean image, competence, national stature, and ability to broaden Ford's political

60

base (because Richardson was seen as a leader of the liberal wing of the Republican Party, whereas Ford was a moderate). Richardson's long association with the Nixon administration was the only strike against him.

Robert Hartmann, who had been Ford's Chief of Staff when Ford was Vice President and who now served as counselor to the President, prepared his recommendations. If Ford intended to run for his own full term in 1976, then he should select Rockefeller, Donald Rumsfeld, or George H.W. Bush. On the other hand, advised Hartmann, if Ford wanted to select a Vice President with the idea of positioning that person to run for the Presidency in 1976, then he should consider Bush, Melvin Laird, or Richardson. Only George H.W. Bush was on both lists. On Saturday morning, August 17, Ford secluded himself in the Oval Office to make his choice. Studying the chart of strengths and weaknesses prepared by Harlow, he made his decision within one hour. Nelson Rockefeller would be the next Vice President.

Historic events had forced President Nixon to leave office and resulted in Ford's unexpected rise to office. Because of this, Ford initially intended to make only minor changes in the Cabinet for the sake of continuity. William Scranton, a former Governor of Pennsylvania and an influential Republican, wrote to Ford to report that he had spoken with Richardson, who was very interested in having a meaningful position in the new administration. The possible positions that Scranton and Richardson had discussed included special assistant to the President for the National Security Council, negotiator at the Strategic Arms Limitations Talks (SALT), head of the Office of Management and Budget (OMB), and director of the Domestic Council. "In short," wrote Scranton, "Elliot seems to be far more interested in being involved in important programmatic work than he is in titles and honors. That speaks well for him and I think gives you a golden opportunity to employ his many talents in useful ways."

On September 8, Ford announced that he was pardoning Richard Nixon of all crimes. America needed to move beyond Watergate, he said. The crisis was consuming too much time and energy.

Shortly before Ford's controversial pardon of the former President, Richardson met with reporters from *The Wall Street Journal*. Over lunch,

61

Richardson told the reporters that the best way to handle the continuing investigations would be for Ford, with the blessing of Congressional leaders, to allow the new special prosecutor to complete his case against Nixon. The government could then tell Nixon that it would not pursue further prosecution in return for a statement by the former President acknowledging his culpability. The idea of using this discretion to decline prosecution would be a better solution than an outright pardon, which denied the nation a sense of closure. Actual prosecution, after all, would serve no purpose except to lay a foundation for sending Nixon to prison. Richardson later regretted that he had not presented his idea to Ford prior to the President's announcement of the pardon (see Appendix C).

Ford decided to place Richardson in one of the most prestigious diplomatic assignments available, Ambassador to the Court of St. James (in Great Britain). He greatly respected Richardson's talents and had been appalled by Nixon's treatment of Richardson in the Saturday Night Massacre. On January 9, 1975, he announced that Richardson would replace Philadelphia publisher Walter H. Annenberg, who had held the post since 1969, and wished to resign. Although Ambassadorial nominations usually are not accompanied by Presidential statements, Ford took this opportunity to comment, "I warmly welcome Elliot Richardson back into the service of our country and I am confident that he will represent America with the highest distinction."

A column by James Reston in the February 28, 1975 *New York Times* discussed the new appointment. He wrote of Richardson, "in many ways, he is the most interesting figure on the American political scene today, maybe better qualified to be President in the last years of the seventies than most candidates now in the race." Although Reston was convinced that the "quiet, thoughtful, and articulate" Richardson would make a good ambassador, he regretted that being in London would effectively take Richardson out of the race for the Republican nomination in 1976. Upon his departure for London, Richardson announced that he would enter the race only if President Ford decided not to seek his own full term.

In early March, Richardson and his wife, Anne, moved into Winfield

House, the American Ambassador's residence, a brick mansion situated on twelve acres of lawns and gardens in London's Regent Park. The Richardsons' oldest son, Henry, was now a student at Harvard, their daughter, Nancy, was a student at Princeton, and their youngest son, Michael, age fourteen, stayed behind in Washington, where he was attending a private school. The Richardsons decided that it was best not to make Michael change schools, since they realized that their stay in London probably would not last long.

Before leaving Washington, Richardson had arranged with the British Ambassador to the United States to exchange use of their fishing club memberships. Sir Peter Ramsbothan would use Richardson's stretch of water along the Maryland-Pennsylvania border and Richardson could fish on the Itchin in Hampshire. The majority of Ambassador Richardson's free time, however, was spent working on his book, since he had finished only two-thirds of the manuscript before leaving the Wilson Center.

During his first month as Ambassador, Richardson spoke at his first major function, the Pilgrims' Society dinner at the Savoy Hotel in London. He told the crowd of four-hundred that Anglo-American relations had never been better. Richardson said, "Advice, response, suggestion, consultation between trusting friends who know one another's virtues and faults, and who are instinctively searching for the same patterns for the future are great restoratives, and give heart to both our countries when we are faced with the increasing problems and tensions in the world." The Ambassador told a writer from *The New Yorker* magazine that he was working on his book while traveling in trains and cars, was spending weekends on it, and often stayed up until 2 a.m. writing. "The book is generally concerned with the relationship of the individual to government," he told the reporter during the interview in the upstairs library, one of the few rooms in the house reserved for the Richardsons' private use. Richardson read a poem he had written as a medic in France. "Well, not a very good poem," he admitted, "but at least technically it's a pretty good sonnet." [3]

Although they were far from home, the Richardsons had brought with them many things to remind them of home. Their residence was decorated with paintings that Anne had borrowed from museums in Washington,

Philadelphia, and Boston. A large Chinese paper screen, a gift from Elliot to Anne celebrating the birth of their first child, had been a part of every home where they had lived. A copy of *The Mind and Faith of Justice Holmes*, edited by Max Lerner – the book that Lieutenant Richardson had carried with him throughout WWII – sat on a bookshelf in their new home.

When President Ford announced in June of 1975, that he would, indeed, seek his own full term as President in 1976, Richardson announced that he would not challenge the President in the primaries. Rather, he would actively campaign on Ford's behalf. Commenting on Ford's leadership, Elliot told the press, "It has been clear from the beginning that he is an honest, open, [and] decent man. He has already made important contributions to the restoration of confidence in government by virtue of these qualities." [4]

Meanwhile, the Ambassador enjoyed his duties, which included visits to steel and textile mills, the British Leyland Motor Works, coal mines in Nottinghamshire, a drilling rig in the North Sea, law courts, trade unions, military services, and universities. Anne often accompanied him. Coincidentally, Archibald Cox also found himself in England following Watergate. Before returning to Harvard, Cox spent one year at Cambridge University as a visiting professor. The two Harvard alumni could now meet and chat under less stressful circumstances than in their previous roles.

During one conversation about Watergate, Cox asked Richardson how he had gotten President Nixon to approve Cox's appointment as special prosecutor. It was an excellent question because the President seemed to believe, by the end, that Richardson could not have appointed anyone more objectionable than Cox. "Well, that's easy," Richardson answered. "I didn't consult him."

Richardson explained that the President had told him that he could appoint a special prosecutor and inform him later of his choice, which is exactly what Richardson did. In his view, he had picked the best person for the job. [5]

Cabinet officers always have their portraits painted and then the portraits are hung in places of honor in the office buildings where the officers worked. During one of his business trips back to the United States, Richardson sat for his portrait. The New York artist Everett Raymond Kinstler, with nineteen such portraits to his credit, was selected to paint Richardson's portrait. The June 14, 1976, *People* magazine reported that, during the sitting, the Ambassador amused himself by doodling on London embassy stationery.

At the end of the session, Richardson handed Kinstler his sketch, which turned out to be of the artist. "Frankly," Kinstler joked, "I think I'm a much better artist than you are." Elliot responded in mock horror, "I should hope so!" Kinstler's portrait of Richardson, finished the following year, was hung in the Pentagon, and *People* magazine published Richardson's rendering of Kinstler.

9

RETURNING TO THE CABINET

"He epitomized integrity, dedication and a willingness to serve when called upon by the President or the public." ~ Gerald R. Ford

"... [Richardson] saw work as a service and the opportunity to serve as a precious gift." ~ Richard Darman

On November 3, 1975, President Gerald Ford announced major changes in his Cabinet and the senior level of his administration.

The biggest news involved Vice President Nelson Rockefeller's announcement that he would not be Ford's 1976 running mate. In his memoirs, Ford recalled the competition for the Republican nomination that he faced from the ultra-conservative wing of his party. The liberal Rockefeller, then almost seventy years old, offered to voluntarily withdraw from the ticket. Although Ford did not ask the Vice President to withdraw, he did tell him that serious political problems would be eliminated if Rockefeller announced his decision not to run. "I understand," said Rockefeller, and added, "well, it's probably better that I withdraw." Ford later lamented in his memoirs, "I was angry with myself for showing cowardice in not saying to the ultra-conservatives: It's going to be Ford and Rockefeller, whatever the consequences" [1]

Rockefeller's announcement led to much public speculation about who would replace him on the ticket. Richardson was one of those mentioned as a potential Vice Presidential candidate, but the President had other plans. Still looking for ways to broaden the philosophical base of his Cabinet, Ford asked Richardson to become the Secretary of Commerce. Richardson told Ford that he would accept only if he would play a significant role in the

66

administration. The President agreed.

Richardson was back in Washington by December for his confirmation hearings before the Senate Commerce Committee. Edward Kennedy, the senior Senator from Richardson's home state of Massachusetts, introduced the nominee to the committee. Kennedy repeated a Washington joke that early every morning Cabinet limousines lined up outside of Elliot Richardson's home, their drivers waiting to see which one he got into so they would know which Cabinet position he held that day. [2]

Edward Brooke, the junior Senator from Massachusetts, welcomed Richardson to the hearing. Noting that this was Richardson's fifth Senate confirmation hearing in six years, Brooke commented, "from this we can only conclude that he is either thoroughly incapable of holding down a job, or he is so capable that his many talents make him too valuable to leave him in one post for too long. Obviously, the latter is true." Having known the nominee for many years, Brooke said, he could testify firsthand "to the many fine characteristics which make him truly one of America's most outstanding public servants."

In his statement to the committee, Richardson said that the challenges facing the Commerce Department involved articulating and defending America's economic system, on which so much of the quality of life in the country depended. A healthy and growing economic system was fundamental to improving employment and living standards, to achieving social justice, and to ensuring national defense and international peace. Among the other critical issues Richardson cited was the proper use of national resources. "The protection and promotion of our free enterprise system is essential not simply in narrow economic terms," he told the committee. "It is essential also to the protection of our liberties at home and to the development of a more productive and humane international order."

During the two-hour hearing, Richardson answered fifty-one questions. The December 5, 1975 *New York Times* called his testimony before the committee a "polished and disciplined performance." After his confirmation by the Senate, Richardson became the Twenty-Third Secretary of Commerce and the first person to occupy four different Cabinet posts.

Although not as large as Defense or HEW, Commerce was a big department that included economic affairs, science and technology, oceanographic and atmospheric activities, domestic and international business, maritime affairs, economic development, and minority business development. Richardson had two primary goals as he took over the department. First, focus American industry on the innovations that would accelerate its global competitiveness. Second, expand United States exports.

When he first addressed department employees on February 3, 1976, Richardson's remarks reflected the upcoming bicentennial of the Declaration of Independence. "We are a people who care about each other, about being fair to each other, about each other's quality of life," he said. "And I think it's time, especially as we look backward to the founding of this Republic and look forward to its future, to reaffirm our own confidence in the continuing vitality of the values that we have brought with us over these two-hundred years, and their relevance to our next one-hundred years and beyond that." He concluded, "This is so most fundamentally because we were founded upon a belief in the dignity and significance of each individual. And I cannot conceive of any purpose of any value that will ever supersede those as basic to everything that the civilized society means." [3]

Cabinet members played a larger role in the Ford administration than under Nixon. The day he learned that he would become President, Ford told his colleague Hugh Scott that "accessibility and openness" would be the hallmarks of his administration. It would be important to restore the people's respect for the Presidency, which had been lost following Watergate. [4]

After healing the wounds of Watergate, the economy was President Ford's top priority. He created the Economic Policy Board (EPB) to advise him on all aspects of national and international economic policy. Richardson served on the EPB along with certain other Cabinet members and senior administration officials. This interagency organization was, in Ford's opinion, "the most important institutional innovation of [his] administration." The group met five-hundred and twenty times, an average

68

of almost five times per week. At least one-hundred of their meetings were with the President. [5]

Along with a number of other projects, the President assigned Richardson the task of investigating questionable payments by United States corporations. Ford believed that Richardson was uniquely qualified to perform a sweeping policy review in this delicate field because of his experience at the Departments of Defense and Justice and as Ambassador to Great Britain. The Commerce Department began cooperating with Congress in investigating compliance by American companies with the United States policy against such business practices. Another crucial policy issue that demanded Richardson's attention was the longtime boycott of Israel by Arab nations.

In February of 1976, Richardson appeared on *Face the Nation* to discuss the upcoming Republican Primary, the economy, the Agnew case, and his post at the Commerce Department. Although it was assumed that Richardson would be a natural successor to Kissinger as Secretary of State if Kissinger left that position, Richardson made it clear that he intended to stay at the Commerce Department through 1981, if Ford won the 1976 election.

The first meeting of the newly created business advisory council of the Commerce Department took place in June. Richardson met with representatives of business, academia, labor leaders, and consumer advocates. During the three-hour session, Richardson asked the group whether a company's responsibility is always to the shareholder or whether there is any public interest that transcends that interest. The Reverend Jesse Jackson, the executive director of Operation PUSH (People United to Save Humanity) in Chicago, delivered a "sermon" in which he called on business executives to develop a "broader vision" that encompassed more than just their companies and not to wait for the government to dictate change. *The Washington Post* quoted Richardson as saying "amen" to Jackson's exhortation.

Richardson's book, *The Creative Balance: Government, Politics, and the Individual in America's Third Century*, was published that summer in time for the primary season and November elections. The book review in the August 29, 1976 *New York Times* noted Richardson's dislike of labels and the fact that neither the conservative nor the liberal label fit him. "He is less likely to seek federal solutions than those Democrats who have spent most of their careers in Washington, but unlike the recent Governors who seek the Presidency, he is not traumatized by national government," wrote the reviewer. Describing Richardson as someone with "almost religious fervor to his feelings for the civic virtues," the review pointed out that *The Creative Balance* demonstrated that "whatever his personal goals may be, Richardson has given more serious thought to the processes of governance and knows more about its purposes, functions, and operations than anyone now seeking support for national office." [6]

President Gerald Ford defeated Ronald Reagan for the Republican nomination for the Presidency, and he quickly selected Senator Bob Dole of Kansas as his running mate. Ford felt that he needed a conservative Vice Presidential candidate to balance the ticket and to appeal to the Reagan wing of the party. Richardson worked hard for Ford's reelection. He believed that Cabinet officers, who share the responsibility for a President's policies, should stand up for those policies in political forums. He spoke at fund-raisers for the Republican Party and for candidates, but he refrained from actually soliciting money. Jimmy Carter, a former Governor of Georgia, defeated Ford in the general election by two percentage points, one of the closest Presidential elections ever. [7]

Ford and Richardson had an excellent working relationship, and Richardson was deeply disappointed by Ford's loss. Following the election, he wrote to the President that he should feel good about having waged such a close campaign. "That this occurred despite the legacy of Vietnam and Watergate and an economic recovery that had begun to lag, is a tribute above all to you as a person," Richardson continued. "Your decency, integrity, and wise judgment won the admiration and respect even of those who, at the last moment, reverted to their national party allegiance or who yielded to the notion that it was time for a change."

"When you step down from office in January," he concluded, "it will be with the gratitude of all the American people for your contributions to the restoration of confidence in the government, the economy, and, above all, in ourselves." [8]

On January 20, 1977, Jimmy Carter was sworn into office and Elliot returned to private life. His next job, however, was not far off.

10

LAW OF THE SEA

"His conviction that nations could address transnational problems despite clashing interests and often fierce rhetoric animated his participation at the Law of the Sea conference." ~ Vivek Viswanathan

The United Nations initially convened a Law of the Sea Conference in 1958, resulting in four treaties. The second conference was launched in 1960, and it failed by one vote to reach a determination on nations' territorial seas. The Third Law of the Sea Conference in 1973, met as a legislative assembly of one-hundred and fifty-six nations to settle international disputes relating to the oceans.

There were many issues facing the delegations as they met in Geneva twice a year for extended periods and again as they worked on the issues in their respective countries. Freedom of the seas was controversial because some coastal nations were interested in extending the historic three-mile limit beyond their shores to twelve miles. In straits which are less than twenty-four miles wide, neutral states would lose their right to navigate critical passages if two facing coastal states instituted such boundaries. Some nations had even considered extending their territories to two-hundred miles. The United States was concerned about preserving the freedom of movement of America's commercial fleet, and the possibility that United States naval forces might lose their ability to maneuver freely on the high seas became a critical issue to the Defense Department.

Cyrus R. Vance became the new Secretary of State in 1977, under President Jimmy Carter. When Vance had to select someone to serve as special representative of the President and chief of the United States delegation to the Law of the Sea Conference, he did not have to look far. Vance and Richardson had been friends for many years and, like Richardson, Vance was a lawyer who had served in several top government posts.

Vance later recalled that when he was faced with the need to find someone to head the United States delegation to the Law of the Sea Conference, "To me there was only one person to take hold of that and really lead it because it is probably one of the most difficult tasks that anybody has ever had put before them." [1]

Vance called Richardson and offered him the job, and Richardson readily accepted. Richardson was one of only a few Republicans offered high-level jobs in the Carter administration. Secretary Vance recalled later that he knew that Richardson would not allow party politics to prevent him from doing important work, and that Richardson regarded representing the United States at the Law of the Sea Conference as critically important work. Richardson later commented that this was his longest and most demanding tour of duty in any government job. [2]

Elliot Richardson made the by-now-familiar trip to Capitol Hill for his third confirmation hearing before the Senate Committee on Foreign Relations. His experience as Undersecretary of State and Ambassador to Great Britain would be essential for this delicate diplomatic post, as would his legal skills and experience at the Department of Defense and the Department of Commerce. On February 24, 1977, the nominee made his opening statement and answered dozens of questions about his thoughts on the Third Law of the Sea Conference, which was entering its fourth year. There had been four previous heads of the United States delegation, and all had been frustrated in their attempts to reach agreement on a treaty that the United States could accept.

Easily confirmed by the full Senate, Richardson left the following week for Geneva, Switzerland, the site for the conference. Representing the United States in the negotiations was a challenging task even for someone of Richardson's caliber. Martin Mayer, in his book, *The Diplomats*, describes the Law of the Sea Conference as a form of four-dimensional chess, because of the complicated nature of the negotiations.

Another issue faced by the Law of the Sea Conference was the development of seabed resources. The natural treasures found on the bottom of the ocean belonged equally to all nations of the world.

Cyrus Vance knew that Richardson's personal style would complement his professional qualifications for such complex work. Ambassador Richardson arrived in Geneva with the advantage of being a recognized leader. Vance recalls that negotiators "were willing to work with him to try and find solutions." Moreover, Richardson "had a splendid quality of being able to articulate what the issues were and how to deal with them with an understanding and in a clear way that gave him sort of a special leadership quality," Vance said. Richardson was patient and "willing to work through problems that took a lot of time and effort." [3]

Richardson thought that he knew a great deal about the art of negotiation going into the conference, but the first few weeks were an education for him. Negotiation is a matter of "convincing the other guy that what you have to offer is worth more than he realized and that he doesn't have much time to get it, while simultaneously convincing him that what he's offering is worth less to you than he thought and that you have all the time in the world," Richardson reflected later. [4]

The conference was the largest and most complex international negotiation that had ever been held. In the eyes of many participants, this was the most important peacetime diplomatic effort since the creation of the United Nations. The United States delegation, which ranged from forty to one-hundred and ten staff members, was one of the largest at the conference. The conference consisted of eighteen committees working in the following six official languages: English, French, Spanish, Arabic, Russian, and Chinese. Formal sessions were translated simultaneously into all member languages, while written translations were made overnight. Work was divided among three main committees. The first covered seabed issues, the second covered traditional maritime law, and the third covered pollution and scientific research.

William Wertenbaker, in a lengthy article about the conference in *The New Yorker* magazine, summarized the negotiations as a debate over scarce resources, "a conference on property and ownership." Diplomats wrestled with issues involving food, oil, energy, minerals, environmental preservation, and freedom of navigation. The conference tried to "bring

74

order and law where none existed or where customs were no longer respected and countries had begun to squabble." [5]

Ambassador Richardson, representing the major power at the conference, operated mostly behind the scenes and frequently made proposals through other delegates. Richardson's doodling on paper was so loud that it could sometimes be heard in the background as the United States stated its position. Mayer observed that Richardson "kept himself sane through the years of negotiations by drawing hundreds of thousands of beautiful owls with a blue felt-tip pen on yellow legal pads." [6]

Richardson became known as outgoing and friendly during the negotiations, offering his assistance even when United States interests were not at stake. The American delegation earned a reputation at the conference for its willingness to compromise when necessary and its openness to new ideas. Ambassador Richardson's style had a transforming influence on the conference, according to several observers. He was held in such high regard that other delegates would work hard to bring about compromises proposed by the United States. Richardson was responsible for arranging some of the conference's most important agreements. Wertenbaker reported, "some delegates felt that since Richardson's appointment to the conference he had, particularly by overcoming distrust of the United States, more influence on the conference than any other delegate." [7]

Richardson spoke at the Washington Press Club in March of 1979, on the topic of "Law of the Sea: A Test for the United Nations." The Ambassador, now with two years in the position, told the assembled journalists that considerable progress had been achieved toward a treaty, with international delegates agreeing on 90 percent of the more than four-hundred articles making up the text of the treaty. "But saying you are 90 percent of the way toward a global convention is about the same as boasting that you are 90 percent of the way to the top of Mount Everest," he said. "That final 10 percent is fraught with hazard." The most difficult areas still to be agreed upon included the decision-making structure of the International Seabed Authority, limits of the continental shelf with implications for gas and oil rights, conditions governing the conduct of marine scientific research, and mechanisms for the compulsory settlement of disputes. Richardson warned that the effectiveness of the United Nations rested on the success of the Law of the Sea Conference. [8]

The spring 1980 issue of the journal *Foreign Affairs* included an article about the Law of the Sea by Richardson, titled, "Power, Mobility, and the Law of the Sea." The Ambassador wrote that the treaty now being crafted would assure rights of navigation and of over flight free of foreign control, free of substantial military risk, and free of economic or political cost. The United States, he argued, would benefit from strengthening the rule of law. A successful outcome of the conference and widespread adoption of the treaty would extend the rule of law over two-thirds of the Earth's surface, he wrote. "In so doing," he concluded, "it would give powerful encouragement to the determined pursuit of other rational accommodations among the ever more complex issues forced upon the world by the imperious realities of its inescapable interdependence."

Richardson viewed international treaty organizations, conferences, and negotiations such as the Law of the Sea Conference as vital to America's interests as well as to global stability, and he vigorously defended United States engagement in international cooperative efforts against the growing isolationist sentiment in the Republican Party. On July 10, 1980, *The Wall Street Journal* published an opinion piece by Richardson titled, "Fortress America Is Out of Date." His column took on those who argued for less reliance on United States allies, less foreign aid, more indifference to the growing disparity between rich nations and poor, reduced support for international organizations, more emphasis on head-to-head encounters, and less regard for world opinion.

In his column, Richardson wrote, "Our global situation demands a broader, not a narrower international perspective in the formulation and conduct of United States policy." He argued that internationalism was the other face of interdependence. "Its concerns are the economic health of the world community as a whole, a stable global equilibrium, and the strengthening of the rule of law. This nation's enduring, long-range interests coincide with these concerns."

By August of 1980, agreement had been reached on all the major issues facing the conference. A tenth and final meeting was planned to take place in New York, in March and April of 1981, with the goal of completing the negotiations. Meanwhile, Republican Ronald Reagan won the 1980 Presidential Election. Reagan made clear that his administration, unlike the Nixon, Ford, and Carter administrations, would not support the Law of the Sea Conference. Because Richardson had supported George H.W. Bush rather than Reagan in the Republican Primaries, he stepped down from his post so the new administration could appoint its own representative. In November of 1980, Richardson was replaced by his own deputy, George Aldrich.

Although many United States observers believed that America was the largest single beneficiary in terms of territory and resources under the provisions negotiated at the conference, Reagan officials stalled United States participation in the talks. James L. Malone was appointed by Reagan to replace Aldrich. On March 9, 1981, the United States delegation shocked conference representatives with the news that the United States had no immediate plans to continue negotiating. [9]

Also on March 9, Richardson fired off a letter to the editor of *The Wall Street Journal* responding to an opinion piece that used the Law of the Sea treaty as an example of United States policy failing to oppose developing nations' quest for a new international economic order, thus playing into the hands of "Third World ideologues." Richardson wrote that the Law of the Sea draft treaty embodied balanced and acceptable compromises "that emerged from tough and protracted battles between the conflicting ideologies and interests of both sides." He argued that this would not have been possible if the United States team had not "fought tenaciously and articulately on behalf of the free enterprise system and its benefits for the world community as a whole."

By 1982, the conference did succeed in securing the sixty votes necessary for ratification and after 12 years of negotiations, 160 countries agreed to the treaty. Although the administration agreed with all provisions except those involving deep-seabed mining, President Reagan decided against signing the final treaty.

Despite the lack of United States support, the conference and the negotiation process were significant. "There is no better example of the process by which universal rules become accepted than the evolution of the Law of the Sea," Richardson wrote. Even before the treaty was signed, the negotiations produced major improvements, since many countries that accepted the initial stipulations actually put them into effect immediately, without waiting for the treaty to be ratified. Although the United States did not directly participate in the final treaty, the treaty clearly benefitted the international community including America.

The new treaty preserved and expanded the freedom of passage, provided protection from pollution for the ocean environment, provided protection against overexploitation of sea life, and created the world's first world organization for managing global resources. According to Wertenbaker, the treaty "created an elaborate system of compulsory settlement of disputes in order to preserve and strengthen the agreements reached. The enforcement provisions were considered a breakthrough in international agreements." [10]

The conference proved that a world of more than one-hundred and fifty countries could achieve long-range solutions to complex problems. "No small group of nations acting on its own," said Richardson, "could deal with any of the truly serious problems of the foreseeable future." The Third Conference of the Law of the Sea, powerfully influenced by Elliot Richardson, thus became a model for future negotiations on worldwide conventions. [11]

11

LEGACY

"[Richardson] was "a national resource." ~ Jonathan Moore

"...the greatest public servant any of us will have the opportunity to meet."
~ Richard Darman

Elliot Richardson was sixty years old when he completed his assignment for the Carter administration. Although it was his last full-time government appointment, it was not the end of his public service. As his old boss Felix Frankfurter often said, citizenship is a democracy's highest office. The Supreme Court Justice would have been proud of his former clerk, who spent the last two decades of his life serving the nation and the world as an elder statesman.

Richardson returned to the practice of law as a senior partner at the Washington, D.C., law firm Milbank, Tweed, Hadley, and McCloy, where he specialized in international litigation. His principal outside interest was the United Nations Association of the United States, of which he served as chair and President, and later as co-chair (with Cyrus Vance) of the association's National Council. He was a charter member of both the American Academy of Diplomacy and of the Council on Ocean Law, and served as longtime chairman of the latter.

In 1981, Richardson and his wife traveled to India, where he gave three lectures, two in Bombay and one in Delhi, as the honored speaker in the Sir Dorab Tata Memorial Lectures. The master of ceremonies, N.A. Palkhivala, told one of the gatherings that Richardson had been invited to deliver the prestigious lectures because he has "an exceptionally well-furnished mind, a comprehensive and comprehending intellect," and has "read about and pondered over problems which concern the human race." [1]

In one of the lectures (published collectively the following year as *The Uses*

79

and Limitations of Law), Richardson told the audience, "The more I have seen of life and government, and of the problems besetting the world, the more I am struck by the importance of the power of imagination." He spoke about the challenge politicians and statesmen face in stopping aggression and how they should receive training in child psychology. There was a strong similarity between the behavior of nations and the behavior of small children, Richardson observed. "Nations are allowed to be, indeed expected to be, touchy, proud, resentful, and mean in a degree that would not be tolerated in an adult. And so the traditional role of statesmen, the role magnified by historians, has, therefore, been that of coping with, and containing, the noisy demands to which these nationalistic traits have given rise." [2]

Richardson sought, but did not win, the Republican nomination for United States Senate in his home state of Massachusetts, in 1984. Although he favored holding down spending, he told voters that new sources of revenue would have to be found to deal with the out-of-control federal budget deficit. His opponent, Raymond Shamie, used Richardson's reasoning to brand him as a candidate who favored tax increases, a charge that ultimately cost Richardson the primary by nearly twenty-five points. This loss hit Richardson hard, but did not derail his commitment to public life. John Kerry defeated Shamie in the election.

On March 18, 1986, Richardson spoke at the Fourth Presidential Library Conference held in Ann Arbor, Michigan, home of the Gerald R. Ford Presidential Library. His talk focused on the power entrusted by citizens to their elected Representatives. He told the crowd, "Although we, the people, have delegated limited responsibilities to those who hold public office in the interest of all of us, we, nevertheless, retain ultimate responsibility. We cannot delegate it; it belongs to us. We may fulfill it well or poorly, but still we have it."

Richardson published an opinion piece in the November 20, 1987 *Wall Street Journal* titled, "Civil Servants: Why Not the Best?" In his editorial, Richardson disputed the view that government should be content with employing competent people, when the business community seeks out the best and most talented. The country needed better motivated, better trained, better qualified, and better paid public servants than ever before, he argued. Society treated public servants, together with teachers, ministers, and others with honorable but low-paid callings, as the beneficiaries of a "high level of psychic income," he wrote. He argued that the prestige of public service was declining with changes such as the tendency for government career service jobs to go to unqualified political appointees.

To combat this erosion, Richardson and others formed the National Commission on Public Service to build public awareness of the "essentiality of the career services to carry out the national agenda, promote measures for strengthening the morale and efficiency of government employees at all levels, encourage the pursuit of excellence by government workers themselves, and make government a more attractive and accessible career choice for young people." [3]

In 1988, Richardson served as a member of a United Nations Commission monitoring elections in Namibia. The following year, he assumed two other diplomatic posts. He accepted an assignment as personal Representative of the United Nations Secretary General to help monitor the elections in Nicaragua. President George H.W. Bush appointed Richardson as his special Representative for an assistance initiative in the Philippines. President Bush said his appointment "of one of our most preeminent statesmen, Ambassador Elliot Richardson, as my personal representative for the initiative shows the priority we accord to its success." [4] Following the Persian Gulf War, Richardson visited Iraq in 1991, as a member of a United Nation's humanitarian mission. The following year, he chaired a working group on ethics in government. In June of 1994, he traveled to England and France for the fiftieth anniversary of the D-Day landing at Normandy.

A longtime admirer of Franklin D. Roosevelt, Richardson was honored on the 50th anniversary of FDR's death at Roosevelt's "Little White House" in Warm Springs, Georgia, on April 12, 1995. Addressing a crowd of dignitaries that included President Bill Clinton and former President Jimmy Carter, Richardson recalled the agonies of the nation in deciding whether to intervene on behalf of the Allies fighting Germany in Europe. He also remembered how Roosevelt led the way for assisting the Allied cause.

"But the striking thing now is that as we look back, we don't think very often of Franklin Delano Roosevelt as a politician," Richardson said. "What is politics, after all, but a process by which competing values are resolved in the general interest? If you can solve a problem by calculation, by cost-benefit analysis, by any purely rationale process, it doesn't need to reach the politicians." Elected office holders, who represent the American people, "have to find a way to contribute to a solution that can in the long term be supported and will in the long term contribute to the general interest."

In 1996, Richardson published *Reflections of a Radical Moderate*, which focused on the three things he knew best: government, citizenship, and politics. He attacked the destructive influence of cynicism and praised the positive influence of moderation. "For me," he wrote, "moderation is not a fighting faith but a faith worth fighting for. My commitment to it is passionate, uncompromising, and deep-rooted – hence, radical."

Addressing the Council for Excellence in Government's John C. Whitehead Forum in 1998, Richardson laid out the following "Four Easy Steps for Building Trust in Government." First, define the problems that we believe government should be called upon to try to solve. Second, identify the most cost-effective ways of dealing with the problems. Third, evaluate whether or not the remedy actually works. Fourth, market the credible, cost-effective solutions that have been identified and assessed. "If you know what works, then you've got to get the word out," he stated." Richardson believed it was necessary to build a broad consensus in supporting these steps:

> The most valuable attitude a politician or bureaucrat can bring as a Presidential appointee to an ongoing institution of government is the understanding that you have to learn – learn what the functions and responsibilities are, who are the people, what are their capabilities, what are their functions. You have to learn what to delegate, how much to delegate. And, of course, you have to begin to try to understand the issues that are presented to that department or agencies, starting with those that are most immediately urgent. And

then try to gain perspective as time permits for the longer-term and larger issues.

On December 1, 1998, the Judiciary Committee of the United States House of Representatives called upon Richardson, the only American to serve in the three legal posts of United States attorney, state Attorney General, and United States Attorney General, to testify. The committee was investigating charges brought by Whitewater special prosecutor Kenneth Starr against President Bill Clinton and weighing whether to recommend to the full House the impeachment of the President. The committee wanted Elliot Richardson's thoughts on the matter.

"The initial wrongdoing was not criminal," Richardson said, and it "did not, in contrast to that of Richard Nixon, entail the abuse of power. Given a President's unique status as a Chief Executive deriving his authority from a majority vote of the American people, a President's crimes or misdemeanors should, in order to justify his removal, be higher than those at issue here," he argued. What the House Committee should recommend to the full House, urged Richardson, was a course of action less destructive than impeachment, namely, censure. It would be a mistake, he said, for the House to vote for impeachment with so many Representatives believing that the President's actions did not warrant conviction by the Senate.

However, the House of Representatives did vote to impeach President Bill Clinton, and by January of 1999, the Senate, as well as the country, was locked in debate on the merits of conviction. The January 25, 1999 *Washington Post* published a letter to the editor from Richardson, in which he attacked the idea of the Senate calling its own witnesses. The House had placed before the Senate, and the American people, the Starr Report, a thick volume summarizing years of investigation of the President's actions. What would be gained by the Senate starting over with witnesses now? "At the end of the day," Richardson wrote, "individual Senators will have to vote yes or no on only one question. Do either or both of the House's charges against Bill Clinton demand his removal from the office to which the American people twice have elected him? To put the same question another way, do perjury and obstruction of justice directed to the concealment, not of abuse of power, but of a private sexual relationship rise to the level of

'High Crimes and Misdemeanors'?" Richardson's point of view was upheld in the final Senate vote clearing Clinton.

Elliot Richardson's career offers many lessons in leadership. He was quick to share his successes at every level with those who surrounded him. His presence improved morale at the departments he headed, and people enjoyed working for him. One technique he used to motivate subordinates was to bring those who worked on a project to the meeting where it was being proposed. They could then see their boss defend the results of their labor and, if their recommendations were turned down, they understood why.

With every change in top leadership during the Nixon and Ford administrations, there was speculation about which job Richardson would land. Richardson was sensitive to the constant speculation about his career path, and always insisted that he never took a job as a way to get to any future post. As he learned early on from Felix Frankfurter, work hard at what you are doing and enjoy it.

In an interview for the November 10, 1975 *New Yorker* magazine conducted while Richardson was serving as Ambassador to Great Britain, the correspondent listed Richardson's predecessors in that post. Four became Presidents, two became Vice Presidents, and six became Secretaries of State. When he asked Richardson which of those jobs he would be most interested in, the Ambassador replied that "it wasn't a matter of being interested, but what you would do to get it." "Yes," Richardson said, he would like any of those jobs, "but I'm not doing anything about it. My behavior is actuated by, I think, an attempt to keep closely in focus an interest in the job to be done for its own sake." [5]

In *Reflections of a Radical Moderate*, Richardson explained that making decisions was easy. The harder part was persuading others, like department colleagues, the White House, outside groups, the press, Congress, or the public, to go along with the decisions. Therefore, building consensus and generating support for ideas were leadership skills that he sought to master throughout his career. Doing the right things "is not ordinarily difficult," he wrote. The key to dealing with most problems "is to stick with the merits and persist in seeking the best and most workable approach." [6]

Reflecting on Richardson's decision-making style, Gerald Ford wrote that it was almost "thoughtful deliberation," and that at times "it was too slow a process." In her summary of Richardson's career in the book, *Political Profiles*, Margaret J. Wyzomirski observed, "If his career demonstrated anything, it would seem to be that in an age of increasing specialization, there is still a prominent place for the intelligent generalist." His admirers were fascinated by his seemingly endless ability to fill any key post in government and tackle any assignment. [7]

In a chapter that Richardson contributed to Phillip Berman's 1986 book titled, *The Courage of Convictions*, Richardson wrote that growing up in a family of doctors taught him about the meaning of service. "The experience of government service has, for me, been a deeply rewarding way of seeking to create fragments worth gathering up. The effort has confirmed my conviction that the key to individual completeness lies in giving and sharing. I feel lucky to have so often been called upon to do my utmost in causes whose outcome has meant so much to so many." [8]

Richardson's reputation extended into the international arena. Ambassador N. A. Palkhivala of India commented that Richardson "has set standards of decency and integrity in public life which have been rarely equaled and never surpassed."

Kenneth W. Thompson, editor of *Portraits of the American Presidents*, wrote in the volume on the Nixon Presidency, "Perhaps a one-sentence introduction is to say that Elliot Richardson, over recent decades, has continued the great tradition of Robert Lovett, Henry Stimson, Clark Clifford, and that handful of Americans who contributed selflessly and with imagination to the tasks of American government in critical periods in our history." Richardson replied to this "one-sentence introduction" that he had to disclaim the use of the word selflessly because "I so much enjoyed public service that, had I the resources, I would have been quite willing to pay for the opportunity to hold some of the jobs I've had." [9]

R. Gordon Hoxie, the longtime President of the Center for the Study of the

Presidency, included Richardson in his list of exemplary Cabinet members in United States history, along with George Marshall, Dean Acheson, Averell Harriman, Robert Lovett, and Cyrus Vance.

Integrity is a word commentators often use when reflecting on Elliot Richardson's long career of public service. He made good on his yearbook promise to pursue politics and performed in a way that clearly showed the virtue of politics – hence the title of this short biography. Although he performed with excellence in numerous positions, the story of his career is bound to focus on his refusal to obey a Presidential order to fire Archibald Cox. By placing the good of the country ahead of his career, even above his loyalty to the President, he provided a dramatic model of integrity and virtue in action in the political realm. Ideally, he would be equally remembered for his passion for service itself, in both elected and appointed posts.

David Reich, writing a feature for the Unitarian publication, *World*, interviewed Richardson, then seventy-five, and painted the following portrait of the public servant.

> Richardson speaks a little slowly and at times so quietly that you have to strain to catch his meaning, and he occasionally stops to edit himself, but his intellect seems as sharp as ever, and his words come out as polished, almost lapidary prose. The day we met him, he wore a glen plaid suit with a white display handkerchief carefully folded in his breast pocket and often leaned his chair way back as he spoke, his long legs out before him and his brown loafers propped up on the coffee table. Along with his intellect, and almost completely unwrinkled face, he retains a quiet sense of fun. A sly smile begins in the corner of his mouth and slowly spreads across his face whenever something strikes him as comical, as happened more than once in our interview. [10]

While Elliot traveled the globe and wrote about citizenship and public policy issues, Anne Richardson led American literacy efforts. In 1969, she joined the board of directors of Reading Is Fundamental, a literacy organization that strives to instill a love of learning in children. During her years as head of the organization, the number of children helped and the number of volunteers both rose dramatically. Her duties took her across the country and she lobbied on Capitol Hill for increased federal funding. Beginning in 1978, she had also volunteered for Second Generation, a Washington-area residential drug treatment program. Anne died of Alzheimer's disease at the age of sixty-nine on July 26, 1999.

Five months after Anne's death, the seventy-nine-year-old Richardson was hospitalized while visiting family in Boston. He died three days later, on New Year's Eve of 1999, of a cerebral hemorrhage. President Clinton issued a statement calling Richardson "an unparalleled public servant." Lengthy accounts of Richardson's life appeared in the January 1, 2000 editions of *The Boston Globe*, *The Washington Post*, and *The New York Times*, in addition to editorials reflecting on the meaning of his career. *The Boston Globe* commented that he "compiled a resume in public life that may never be equaled short of the White House." *The Washington Post* opined that "he will be remembered as the Attorney General who put country before party or personal ambition." The *Post* editorial continued, "he emerged from each Presidential assignment undefeated by the bureaucracy he encountered, a rare achievement."

David Broder wrote, "Engagement, not resignation, was the keynote of Richardson's extraordinary public life." In a piece titled, "Elliot Richardson's Choice," William D. Ruckelshaus, Richardson's former Deputy Attorney General, reminded the readers of the January 5, 2000 *Washington Post* of the intense situation in which Richardson found himself as Attorney General, handling the Agnew case in addition to Watergate. Just as America's best leaders, such as Washington, Lincoln, and Franklin Roosevelt, surface during times of great need, wrote Ruckelshaus, "Our country is better off because Elliot Richardson lived...[his] life and the choices he made in time of national crisis are a tribute to him and the enduring values of America." Writing in the January 4, 2000 *Boston Globe*, Thomas Oliphant said that Richardson "electrified and transfixed a country desperate for mature, principled leadership."

On January 15, 2000, more than one-thousand people attended a memorial service in Richardson's honor at the National Cathedral in Washington,

D.C. His former assistant, Richard Darman, said that day, "He provided a symbol of public virtue for a society on the edge of cynicism." The Richardson family asked Jonathan Moore, Richardson's longtime Chief of Staff (later an Ambassador and then a professor at Harvard), to read at the service, "The Truly Great," by the British poet Stephen Spender. The poem begins, "I think continually of those who were the truly great," and concludes with the following: "The names of those who in their lives fought for life, Who wore at their hearts the fire's centre. Born of the sun, they traveled a short while toward the sun And left the vivid air signed with their honour."

On January 15, 1998, in a White House ceremony in the East Room, Richardson received the Medal of Freedom from President Bill Clinton. Established in 1963, by President John F. Kennedy, the Medal of Freedom is the highest American civilian award, given to those who have made especially meritorious contributions to the security or national interests of the United States, to world peace, or to cultural or other significant public or private endeavors. Prior to placing the medal around Richardson's neck, President Clinton stated, in part, that Richardson " . . . gave courageous and deeply moral service to our nation as Secretary of Health, Education, and Welfare, Secretary of Defense, Ambassador to the United Kingdom, Secretary of Commerce . . . and, of course, as Attorney General, where, on one difficult Saturday night, he saved the nation from a Constitutional crisis with his courage and moral clarity. No public servant is more beloved by those who have served him. No public servant has shown greater respect for the Constitution he has served."

This is Elliot Richardson's legacy, the life of a talented man of unimpeachable integrity whose lifelong passion was public service in the realms of state, national, and international politics.

Postscript

Two awards continue his legacy: Harvard University's Elliot and Anne Richardson Fellowships and The Elliot Richardson Prize for Excellence in Public Service by the National Academy of Public Administration.

AFTERWORD

This section has been added to this edition, originating as an essay for a 1993 graduate course in professional writing taught by Professor Bradley Hayden at Western Michigan University. It was titled "Elliot Richardson Throughout My Years," and the second draft I've kept all these years is marked with the grade B-A, along with a question about who my audience might be. Dr. Hayden encouraged us to think of an audience for every assignment, believing that if something was worth writing – even for class – it was worth submitting for publication.

I was in my junior year at Western Michigan University in 1976 when I first met Elliot Richardson. As managing editor of the student newspaper, *The Western Herald*, with a fellow coworker at the newspaper – Conrad Sutter – we drove to nearby Benton Harbor to cover Richardson's appearance on behalf of two Republican Congressional candidates. I remember calling the White House from the *Herald* offices to get a press pass only to be told by the switchboard that the Department of Commerce would be the place to call since Richardson was secretary there. Turns out we didn't need passes, but it was exciting to make the calls.

Richardson held a press conference prior to the fundraiser dinner ($150 a plate), held at the Ramada Inn. Once he took his place at the podium, Richardson had a difficult time hearing some of the questions during the press conference. To our surprise, instead of waiting for someone else to handle it, he excused himself and walked over to a nearby party of hotel guests and asked them to please keep the noise down. It appeared beneath a cabinet officer, but we were impressed by his 'take-charge' demeanor.

Already vested with a deep interest in his career, I'd recently bought his new book, *The Creative Balance*. I'd brought it with me, but had left it in the car, too chicken to take it inside to be inscribed. Luckily, and unknown to me, Conrad ran out following the press conference, retrieved the book, and had Richardson sign it during the reception: "To Tom Vance with best wishes, Elliot Richardson, October, 1976" in the typical blue felt-tip pen he was famous for.

89

Richardson was introduced by Congressional Candidate David Stockman, who joked about Elliot's numerous cabinet posts: "Maybe he will find a steady job someday." Following his dinner speech – during which Richardson declared the election will have a "profound effect on the future of this country" – the Commerce Secretary took questions. Either Conrad or I asked him if he planned to remain in the cabinet should President Ford lose the upcoming election to Jimmy Carter. He indicated that yes, he would consider that. It turns out that was a pretty good question, since Richardson ended up being one of the few Republicans to serve in a high level appointment in the Carter administration. Our double-bylined story ran the next day with the headline "Watergate Survivor Speaks on GOP" but didn't mention what we correctly thought was the biggest news.

Two days before Richardson's campaign stop in Michigan my weekly column ran in the *Herald* explaining my support for Ford and insisted that he should have selected Richardson as his running mate, "whose resume in government cannot be topped by any public servant in the country." Meanwhile, I predicted the election wrong, saying that people would stick with Ford, but I had underestimated the cynicism that resulted from the deep wounds of Watergate.

My signed copy of *Creative Balance*, complete with more than 50 markings from numerous readings, became a mini-archive of Richardson memorabilia including the Southwest Michigan Republicans "Victory '76 Dinner" program from that evening and future clippings.

Kathy and I were living in Ansbach, Germany, while I was stationed with the 1st Armored Division – and a month following the birth of our daughter Kelly – I wrote Richardson a letter via Holt, Rinehart and Winston, the publishers of *Creative Balance*. After saying how much I'd enjoyed re-reading his book, I boldly wrote, "I may add that I have always been amazed by your great career of public service and am hoping for a biography to appear sometime. Otherwise, I should be tempted to write one myself!" I don't know if he ever received the letter, but a copy of it went into my autographed copy of his book.

When I was in Professor Hayden's essay writing class in 1993, while working in public affairs at The Upjohn Company – at that point pursuing an MA in English with an emphasis in professional writing, before eventually switching over to an MA in History – he had us share with the class what each of us would do if we won the lottery (the point being, if we didn't have to work). I said how I would write a biography of Elliot Richardson. Having said that, he and my classmates agreed that I would just have to find a way to do that without winning the lottery. The first product of this effort was a 5,635 word article about Richardson's stint as Defense Secretary, which remained unpublished. That led to receiving a $165 research grant by the Gerald R. Ford Presidential Foundation to study their documents about Richardson's service during the Ford years. That led to the opportunity to meet with Richardson in June of 1994 in his office at Milbank, Tweed, Hadley and McCloy on "Eye" Street in Washington, D.C.

I arranged to see Richardson while I was in Washington, D.C., that summer for my two-week Army Reserve duty. Richardson's assistant Marguerite Randolph, called me to say she had to reschedule since a last-minute meeting with the Japanese Ambassador just came up. When I did show up for the rescheduled meeting, I was in my Army uniform. He came out to the lobby to greet me and held his arms out to his sides, as if to say, "Look at you," not expecting to see his visitor in uniform. He began by stating that I had submitted three pages of questions – which three questions did I want to cover? I tried not to ask questions that others had documented, and he discussed his time as Defense Secretary, his years in the Ford Administration, and leadership in general. The hour zoomed by and I left knowing that I had to write about his full life, not just separate components.

A few episodes along this journey. I had the chance to pick up former Carter spokesman Jody Powell at the airport in Kalamazoo for an Upjohn-hosted event, and took the opportunity to ask about Elliot. We discussed *The Creative Balance* and agreed that too few people had read it. Powell said that Richardson (73 years-old) wasn't that visible any longer in Washington, which of course, disappointed me. Meanwhile, I'd heard a story on how *Time* magazine had considered putting

91

Richardson's picture on its October 29, 1973, cover following the Saturday Night Massacre. According to the story, Richardson asked the magazine not to put him on the cover because it would detract from his resignation. The cover ended up featuring photos of Nixon and Cox, with the appearance of a rip or tear between the two photos. I was unsuccessful in confirming this story with Time magazine. Finally, while in Boston on business, and finding myself with a few free hours, I traveled out to Brookline on a commuter train, and then took a cab to Elliot's boyhood neighborhood. I walked by the house he grew up in and walked around the area taking in the history and ambiance. And later, in 2004, I wrote to the United States Postal Service recommending Elliot as the subject for a stamp. I heard back, saying my recommendation was being shared with the Citizen's Stamp Advisory Committee, but sadly – so far – no stamp.

By 1998, I'd shared a 35,000-word draft with Richardson geared for a young adult audience, realizing I didn't have the time or resources for an adult, full-length biography. He wrote the only letter I would receive from him, saying, "he would be delighted to see the book succeed in inspiring an increased interest in politics on the part of young people," but didn't have any "suggestions as to how its value for this purpose might be enhanced." Meanwhile, Everett Raymond Kinstler – the artist who did Richardson's Pentagon portrait – received Richardson's permission in 1997 to share that artwork for this short bio (and it appeared on the cover of the 2000 edition).

The Council for Excellence in Government agreed to make the manuscript available on their website as one of their online publications. That was Dec. 21, 1999, and Richardson was aware that the manuscript was in their hands, but he passed away on New Year's Eve. Former Secretary of State Cy Vance (no relation) had promised to write the foreword once I found a home for the biography. Elva Murphy, his private secretary, wrote on Jan. 10, 2000, saying that Secretary Vance was ill and not able to take on any writing projects.

From 2002 to 2005, I was able to devote a good deal of my studies in my MA in History (with a concentration in biography) to studying Richardson's mentors: his Uncle Harry, Henry Lee Shattuck; Judge Learned Hand, Justice Felix Frankfurter, and Senator Leverett Saltonstall. As I discovered when writing this bio, everyone I contacted about Richardson's life were enthusiastic with their assistance. It was rewarding to see "The Mentors of Elliot Richardson" make the cover of the annual 2006 issue of the *Massachusetts Historical Review* (and thanks to Dr. Henry Richardson for locating some of the photos they used).

When the Council for Excellence in Government dissolved a few years ago, their publications went off-line. I spoke with Don Carr at that point about making this manuscript available through print-on-demand or as an e-book just to have it "out there" and he agreed that would be worthwhile. With Don's passing, it became even more important to move this project along to fill the gap until his book is published. I had the privilege of reading portions of his draft manuscript and I have no doubts that his book will be the definitive biography of Elliot Richardson.

TIMELINE

1920: Born in Boston, Massachusetts

1941: Graduates from Harvard College

1942: Enters the Army during World War II

1947: Graduates from Harvard Law School

1947: Law Clerk for Judge Learned Hand

1948: Law Clerk for Justice Felix Frankfurter

1949: Associate at Ropes and Gray

1952: Marries Anne Francis Hazard

1953: Staffer to United States Senator Leverett Saltonstall

1954: Associate at Ropes and Gray

1957: Assistant Secretary for Legislation at Health, Education, and Welfare

1959: United States Attorney for Massachusetts

1961: Special Assistant to the United States Attorney General

1961: Partner at Ropes and Gray

1965: Elected Lieutenant Governor of Massachusetts

1967: Elected Attorney General of Massachusetts

1969: Under Secretary of State

1970: Secretary of Health, Education, and Welfare

1973: Secretary of Defense

1973: Attorney General

1973: Fellow at Wilson International Center for Scholars

1975: Ambassador to Great Britain

1976: Secretary of Commerce

1976: *The Creative Balance* is published

1977: Chief, United States Delegation, Law of the Sea Conference

1980: Senior Partner at Milbank, Tweed, Hadley, and McCloy

1982: *The Uses and Limitations of Law* is published

1984: Unsuccessful bid for Republican U.S. Senate nomination

1989: Personal Representative of United Nations Secretary-General for Nicaraguan Elections

1989: Special Representative of President of the United States for Multilateral Assistance Initiative for the Philippines

1989: Co-Chair of the National Council of the United Nations Association of the United States of America

1991: Member of United Nations Humanitarian Commission to Iraq

1996: *Reflections of a Radical Moderate* is published

1998: Awarded the Presidential Medal of Freedom

1999: Dies in Boston on New Year's Eve

APPENDIX A

Phone interview with Cyrus Vance, April 24, 1995.

TV: Thank you for taking the time to answer my questions.

CV: Well, I'm delighted to do it, because I'm a great fan and admirer of Elliot's.

TV: Could you comment on your association with Mr. Richardson up to his appointment as Ambassador-at-Large for the Law of the Sea delegation?

CV: I've known Elliot for a long while and have always been a great, great admirer of him and the way he has been able to lead in everything he has put his hand to. He is incredibly bright and extremely able as a leader and as a person who is able to deal wonderfully and effectively with other people and that's reflected in all the various posts he's filled and discharged with such skill. So, I've known him and liked him and admired him for all these many years. And when the time came that we had really to get somebody who could take over as chief of the Law of the Sea delegation, to me there was only one person to take hold of that and really lead it because it is probably one of the most difficult tasks that anybody has ever had put before them. And I think Elliot would tell you the same thing; that that's probably the most difficult job he ever had to do. And he did it with tremendous skill. It made a tremendous difference to us because somebody had to keep that moving in a constructive way despite all of its complexities. Thus, I have been forever grateful to Elliot for having taken on that task and having discharged it with such a valuable contribution.

TV: Are there certain characteristics, skills or special qualities that he brought to the job?

CV: Well, yes, he was a recognized leader and everybody respected him and as such they were willing to work with him to try and find solutions to the problems which were so difficult and complex that faced him in his job with the Law of the Sea. He had a splendid quality of being able to articulate what the issues where and how to deal with them with an understanding and clear way that gave him sort of a special leadership quality. He was patient. He was willing to work through problems that took a lot of time and effort to deal with and he also had the quality of being able to find solutions to problems because, really, his brilliance in dealing with these complex problems.

TV: It must have been a great disappointment that the treaty wasn't followed through by the United States.

CV: It was, yes, but in the end the leadership that he gave to it during that period of time made a tremendous difference.

TV: Your working relationship with him?

CV: Great to work with.

TV: Those working for him?

CV: All admired him, all of them. Somebody who was memorable to work with.

TV: He had so many different positions in government.

CV: That's right. That reflects the admiration and ability that he had to command the various offices that were thrust upon him. I think he and Averell Harriman probably had more positions than anybody else that I know of in at least the last 50, 60, 70 years.

TV: Was it significant that he continued his public service under a Democratic administration?

CV: No, I think he felt that this was a subject of critical importance. He thought he could bring to bear to it the tasks that were going to be required. It didn't make any difference to him that the Democrats were in power at that time. I liked him and we both admired each other; therefore, it was not really at all surprising that he was willing to work with me on this and we found it so congenial.

TV: Previously, the two of you had never worked together?

CV: That's right. We used to play tennis against each other; he and his wife and I and my wife enjoyed those kind of things.

TV: I had the honor of meeting with Mr. Richardson last summer and have gotten great cooperation from lots of people, mostly so far from those in the Ford administration.

CV: You couldn't find a finer, more gifted person than Elliot.

APPENDIX B

Letter to the author by former President Gerald R. Ford, April 7, 1994:

The following is a response to your letter of February 5, requesting answers to questions on Elliot Richardson:

1. Re: Ambassador to Great Britain:

    a) I selected Elliot Richardson for the post in London, because I thought he was well qualified and did effectively represent my Administration.

    b) I have no recollection of why "his duties involving broad European diplomacy" didn't take hold. All I know is that program of Elliot's did not get a favorable response in Europe.

Re: Secretary of Commerce:

    a)   I called Elliot Richardson back from London to take the Cabinet post at Commerce, because of an overall number of changes in the Cabinet as a whole. I did not consider him for the CIA or the Department of Defense.

    b)   Elliot Richardson proved to be a constructive member of the Economic Policy Board. He also worked effectively on the Energy Resource Council and the Cabinet Committee on Ocean's Policy. In every assignment Elliot Richardson performed very well.

    c)   ... leadership style ...

        - I had an excellent personal relationship with Elliot Richardson as a subordinate.

        - Elliot Richardson's decision-making style was almost "thoughtful deliberation." At times it was too slow a process.

        - Elliot Richardson always made a very fair, accurate presentation of a controversial issue.

- Elliot Richardson had reasonably good relationships with other Cabinet Secretaries and White House personnel. I am not sure he was an intimate of any of those individuals, but there was no public disagreement to my knowledge.

1. Re: Potential for service in a second term

    a. Frankly, I had made no plans or commitment to Elliot if I had been elected in November 1976. I was so involved in the election, I had not given the future any in-depth consideration.

    b. If I had been reelected, I wanted Henry Kissinger to stay on as Secretary of State, so I had not given any thought to Elliot Richardson succeeding him.

2. Elliot Richardson had a long and very effective career in public service. He epitomized integrity, dedication and a willingness to serve when called upon by the President or the public.

APPENDIX C

Excerpt from "Elliot Richardson, Oral History," by Richard L. Holzhausen, April 25, 1997, from the Gerald R. Ford Presidential Library (selections from pages 4-5 from the 15-page interview).

Thanks to Archives Technician Elizabeth Druga, Gerald R. Ford Presidential Library and Museum, for her assistance in how to properly cite this entry.

This portion of Holzhausen's interview references President Ford's pardon of former President Nixon. Richardson said, "There is one story I really do want to tell you ... I would like to get this in because I don't think it's ever been told." Richardson explained to Holzhausen that while serving as a U.S. Attorney he had been aware that "we didn't prosecute everyone who might be guilty of something. There existed, in the Department of Justice in general, and among U.S. Attorneys in particular the discretion to decline prosecution."

I thought that the solution that Ford should use in dealing with Nixon was the following: First, he would talk with the attorney general and tell him that he thought the attorney general should see to it that special prosecutor, Leon Jaworski, should complete the investigation of any wrong doing arising out of Watergate and spell out the charges that could have been brought against the former president. He should then ask the attorney general, once this had been done, to meet with the leadership and the chairman of ranking members of the judiciary committees in the House and Senate. The attorney general would say to them, "gentlemen, I have looked at this situation and it strikes me that no useful purpose would be served by proceeding with a trial or indictment against Richard Nixon. The most a judgment of guilty would do would be to lay a foundation for sending him to jail. But he's already paid the supreme penalty of being forced to resign. Of course, if he were indicted, he would have all the rights of any defendant, and the proceedings could drag on for years. I submit to you that proper causes here in these circumstances since the judgment would have no affect other than to create a foundation for a jail sentence, I submit to you that the result should be that we, the Department of Justice, decline prosecution...

Now, I'm certain that the leadership of both parties and both branches as well as the Judiciary Committee members, would have said, sure…

[*Richardson explained to Holzhausen that he was working out details of this recommendation and getting feedback to the concept at a lunch meeting*].

Well, damned if the President didn't pardon Nixon on the Sunday between that Thursday lunch and the Tuesday breakfast. What I should have done as soon as I thought of this was to go directly to Ford and put it to him. Of course, I was out of office then … But I think if I had done that and he had not pardoned Nixon … that we would have been spared all the fallout of the pardon. I think again, Ford would clearly have been reelected. Boy, I have been kicking myself ever since…

NOTES

This edition has not been updated with research conducted since 2000; however, I have used sources published since then for some of the opening chapter quotes and supporting information in this reference section.

Opening quote on page viii, Vivek Viswanathan, *Crafting the Law of the Sea: Elliot Richardson and the Search for Order on the Oceans, (1977-1980)*, 2009, 6. Viswanathan received Harvard University's 2009 John Dunlop Undergraduate Thesis Prize in Business and Government. His thesis is available at: http://www.hks.harvard.edu/m-rcbg/students/dunlop/2009-Viswanathan%20Thesis.pdf

Back cover quote from the *Iliad*: Judge Learned Hand gave Richardson a photograph of himself inscribed with this passage from Homer's *Iliad*, "Now, though numberless fates of death beset us which no mortal can escape or avoid, let us go forward together, and either we shall give honor to one another, or another to us." Since Archibald Cox had also clerked with Judge Hand, Richardson recited this passage on the phone with Cox during the Saturday Night Massacre when discussing their fates; Richardson's resignation and Cox's firing. See Richardson, *The Creative Balance* [45].

Scholarship since 2000, in addition to those sources cited in the Author's Note, includes the works of Geoffrey Kabaservice: *The Guardians: Kingman Brewster, His Circle, and the Rise of the Liberal Establishment* (Henry Holt and Company, 2004) features Richardson along with Cyrus Vance, McGeorge Bundy, Paul Moore, Jr., and John Lindsay. He writes, "These were the last of the Wise Men. Their legacy is still with us." [13]. His *Rule and Ruin: The Downfall of Moderation and the Destruction of the Republican Party from Eisenhower to the Tea Party* (Oxford University Press, 2012) also discusses Richardson.

For the 40th anniversary of Nixon's resignation, Elizabeth Drew's *Washington Journal: 1973-1974* published in 1975 has been reissued as *Washington Journal: Reporting Watergate and Richard Nixon's Downfall* (Overlook, New York, 2014), with a new afterword. The new edition is dedicated "To those who rose to the occasion."

The Association for Diplomatic Studies and Training conducted an interview with Richardson that went online after the completion of this biography in 2000: http://www.adst.org/OH%20TOCs/Richardson,%20Elliot.toc.pdf

The Elliot L. Richardson Papers at the Library of Congress consist of 165,000 items. The 145-page finding aid was completed in 2012, prepared by Allan Teichroew and Brad E. Gernand, and revised and expanded in 2013 by Karen Linn Femia with the assistance of Thomas Bigley, Jeffry Bryson, and Dan Oleksiw.

1: Saturday Night Massacre

Chapter heading quote:
Mary McGrory, speaking of Richardson, in Donald A. Carr's entry on Richardson in *Yale Biographical Dictionary of American Law*, 2009, 457.

1. Gormley, Kenneth. *Archibald Cox: Conscience of a Nation*, Reading, Massachusetts: Addison-Wesley, 1977, 365-366.

2. Richardson, Elliot, in *Courage of Convictions*, edited by Phillip L. Berman, New York: Ballantine, 1986, 207.

2: The Early Years

Chapter heading quote:
Rod Skinner, "Some Are Born to Greatness: Elliot L. Richardson," *Milton Academy Magazine*, 2000, 2.

Commentary:
According to Donald Carr, the young Richardson "particularly admired the Republican Secretary of State, Henry L. Stimson. He would adopt Stimson's maxim: When in doubt, march toward the guns" (*The Scribner Encyclopedia of American Lives*, vol. 5, 1997-1999, edited by Kenneth T.Jackson, New York, 2002, 480). Read more about Henry L. Stimson, one of Richardson's early heroes, in the four-page profile, "Laird of Woodley" in *The New Yorker* by Henry F. Pringle, October 4, 1930. Also see *The Colonel: The Life and Wars of Henry Stimson, 1867-1950* by Godfrey Hodgson, 1990. The Stimson Center, a Washington, D.C., nonprofit and nonpartisan think tank (www.stimson.org) carries on Stimson's belief in "pragmatic solutions" for global security.

1. Lyndon, Christopher. "Richardson and Justice," *The New York Times*, May 20, 1973, reprinted in *The New York Times Biographical Edition*, May 1973, 882.

2. Szulc, Ted. "The Smile on the Face of Elliot Richardson," *Esquire*, July, 1974, 77.

3. Reich, David. "Profile: Elliot Richardson: A Late Encounter with Mr. Clean," *World* Unitarian Universalist magazine, Jan/Feb 1997, 22; Lyndon, Richardson and Justice; Richardson, Elliot. *The Uses and Limitations of Law*, New Delhi: Tata McGraw-Hill, 1982, 10.

4. Lyndon, Richardson and Justice, 883; Reich, 22. For more on Shattuck, see John T. Galvin, *The Gentleman Mr. Shattuck: A Biography of Henry Lee Shattuck 1879-1971*, Boston: Tontine Press, 1996.

5. Richardson, Elliot. Foreword to *The World of Roger Tory Peterson: An Authorized Biography* by John C. Devlin and Grace Naismith, New York: Times Books, 1977, xi-xii.

6. Richardson, Elliot. "Rara Avis: Roger Tory Peterson, Naturalist and Artist," *Yankee*, September 1995 (No. 59), 50.

7. Richardson, *World of Roger Tory Peterson*, xii – xiii.

8. Richardson, Elliot. *Reflections of a Radical Moderate*, New York: Pantheon Books, 1996, 158.

9. Richardson, Elliot. *The Creative Balance: Government, Politics, and the Individual in America's Third Century*, New York: Holt Rinehard and Winston, 1976, 149.

10. Richardson, in *Courage of Convictions*, 206; Lyndon, Richardson and Justice, 882.

11. Richardson, *Creative Balance*, 347; Richardson, in "Legends in the Law: A Conversation with Elliot L. Richardson," *Bar Report*, District of Columbia Bar Association, February/March 1995, 6.

12. Richardson, Elliot. "Mutual Regard: Alumni Exchange Reflections on the School," *Harvard Law Bulletin Index* (42, No. 3), SP 1991, 7.

13. Richardson, Elliot. "Rule in Cox's Case," *Harvard Law School Bulletin*, Fall 1982, 8; Richardson, Mutual Regard, 7.

14. Richardson, in *Bar Report*, 6. For more on Hand, see *The Spirit of Liberty: Papers and Addresses of Learned Hand*, edited by Irving

Dilliard, Chicago: University of Chicago Press, 1977. Also see Gerald Gunther, *Learned Hand: The Man and the Judge*, New York, 1994. According to Ken Gormley, "Hand's influence on American law was based in large part on the addresses and opinions that flowed from his fountain pen. But it was based as well upon the silent array of clerks that he molded during his gruff, playful, moody years as a federal judge." (*Archibald Cox*, 45).

15. Richardson, in *Bar Report*, 6. For more on Frankfurter, see Liva Baker, *Felix Frankfurter*, New York, 1969.

16. Gormley, 86.

17. Gormley, 87.

18. Richardson, Elliot. "Freedom of Expression and the Function of Courts," *Harvard Law Review*, November 1951,(65, No. 1), 54. Richardson told Tad Szulc that this was still his proudest piece of writing, *The Smile on the Face of Elliot Richardson*, *Esquire*, July 1974, 138.

19. Bart Barnes. "Anne Richardson Dies: Literary Group Leader was Cabinet Spouse," *The Washington Post*, July 28, 1999.

20. *Current Biography*. "Elliot Lee Richardson," Bronx, New York: H.W. Wilson, 1971,343. For more on Saltonstall, see his memoirs *Salty: Recollections of a Yankee in Politics*, as told to Edward Weeks, Boston: Boston Globe, 1976.

3: Politics and Law

Chapter heading quote:
Jonathan Moore, phone interview with the author, May 15, 2004.

Commentary:
Read about Jonathan Moore in "The Kennedy School Rings Thrice," by Steve Nadis, Harvard University's *Kennedy School Magazine*, Autumn, 2011.

1. Richardson, *Creative Balance*, 122.

2. Richardson, *Creative Balance*, 34.

3. Richardson, *Reflections*, 188-189.

4. Richardson, *Reflections*, 192.

5. Richardson, *Creative Balance*, 125.

6. Richardson, *Creative Balance*, 180.

7. Richardson, *Creative Balance*, 22.

4: Foggy Bottom

Chapter heading quotes:
- Summer Gage Whittier, in an undated letter to the author (received in April 2004).
- Geoffrey Kabaservice, *The Guardians: Kingman Brewster, His Circle, and the Rise of the Liberal Establishment*, New York: Henry Holt, 2004, 6.

Commentary:
During his confirmation hearing before the Senate Committee on Foreign Relations to become Under Secretary of State, Richardson was up front about several driving violations he had as a young man, some of which involved speeding and some alcohol. See *Nomination of Elliot L. Richardson to be Under Secretary of State*, U.S. Government Printing Office: Washington, January 15, 1969, 6-10.

1. Senate Committee on Foreign Relations, Nomination of Elliot L. Richardson as Under Secretary of State, January 15, 1969, 2-3.

2. Lydon, Richardson and Justice, 882.

3. Richardson drew tanks and geometric designs during a meeting on May 6, 1970, reflecting the armored cavalry action in progress in Cambodia. Doodle in the possession of the author.

5: Mr. Secretary

Chapter heading quotes:
- Donald T. Bliss, letter to the author, March 2, 2004.
- Geoffrey Kabaservice, *The Guardians*, p. 426. He also noted that: "Only a few weeks after he was sworn in, Richardson rescued Nixon's ambitious welfare reform bill, the Family Assistance Plan, from sure defeat. In a marathon six-day testimony before the mostly hostile Senate Finance Committee, Richardson dazzled the panel with his familiarity with every

clause and subclause of the complex, 153-page bill" (426).

1. *National Journal.* "Elliot Richardson's Tenure as HEW Secretary: Many Defeats and Frustrations, Taken in Spirit of Loyalty," Jan. 6, 1973 (5, No. 1), 8.

2. Richardson, *Creative Balance*, 157.

3. Lydon, Christopher. "The Choice for HEW: Elliot Lee Richardson," *The New York Times*, June 8, 1970, reprinted in *The New York Times Biographical Edition*, April/June 1990 (Vol. 1), 1305.

4. *National Journal*, 8.

5. *The New York Times Biographical Edition*, 1712.

6. Richardson, *Reflections*, 62.

7. *National Journal*, 8; Richardson, *Reflections*, 72.

6: From Defense to Justice

Chapter heading quote:
- John Thomas Smith II, e-mail to the author, February 11, 2004.

Commentary:
Read about John Thomas Smith II in his 2012 book, *Cars, Energy, Nuclear Diplomacy and the Law: A Reflective Memoir of Three Generations*, Rowman & Littlefield, Maryland, 2012. He is also known as J.T. Smith II.

1. Richardson, in *Bar Report*, 7.

2. *Congressional Record*, Senate, January 12, 1973, 1021.

3. *Congressional Record*, Senate, January 12, 1973, 1031.

4. Richardson, *Creative Balance*, 190.

5. *Annual Defense Department Report*, FY 1974, April 10, 1973, 1, 10.

6. Richardson, in McCloud, Bill. *What Should We Tell Our Children About Vietnam?* Norman: University of Oklahoma Press, 1989, 104-105.

7. White, Theodore. *Breach of Faith*, New York: Reader's Digest Press, 1975, 180.

8. Palmer, Bruce, Jr. *The Twenty-Five-Year War: America's Military Role in Vietnam*, Lexington: University Press of Kentucky, 1984, 139, 200.

9. Richardson, *Creative Balance*, 3.

10. Richardson, *Creative Balance*, 4-5.

11. Richardson, *Creative Balance*, 5.

12. Gormley, 235.

13. Gormley, 232, 298, 241.

14. *Congressional Record*, Senate, May 21, 1973, 16203.

7: Making the System Work

Chapter heading quotes:
- James Bennet, "Elliot Richardson: The Longest Day," The Lives They Lived (an annual issue), *The New York Times Magazine*, January 7, 2001, 22.
- Richard Darman. in Spencer S. Hsu, "Washington Honors Elliot Richardson," *The Washington Post*, January 16, 2000.

Commentary:
- On October 11, 1973, Richardson held a press conference on how the Agnew case was settled. The Department of Justice released the 40-page report: "Exposition of the Evidence Against Spiro T. Agnew Accumulated by the Investigation in the Office of the United States Attorney for the District of Maryland as of October 10, 1973." See Elizabeth Drew, *Washington Journal: Reporting Watergate and Richard Nixon's Downfall*, New York: Overlook Duckworth, 2014, 38.
- Read about Richard Darman in "Richard G. Darman, 64, Aide for 5 Presidents, Dies," by Douglas Martin, *The New York Times*, January 26, 2008.
- General Haig and Richardson obviously did not agree on Richardson's stand-off with the President. When I wrote to General Haig for a comment for this book, he responded saying he did not want to offer further comment about Richardson, but he wished me luck with my project – a response that I thought that was very commendable.

1. *Time*. "The Presidential Cleanup Crew," May 14, 1973.

2. Richardson, *Creative Balance*, 129.

3. Cohen, Richard M., and Jules Witcover. *A Heartbeat Away: The Investigation and Resignation of Vice President Spiro T. Agnew*, New York: Viking Press, 1974, 100.

4. Cohen and Witcover, 112.

5. Cohen and Witcover, 127.

6. Haig, Alexander M., Jr. *Inner Circles*, New York: Warner Books, 1992, 352.

7. Haig, 353.

8. Cohen and Witcover, 146.

9. Richardson, *Creative Balance*, 101-102; Haig, 366.

10. Haig, 366.

11. Nixon, Richard M. *The Memoirs of Richard Nixon*, New York: Warner Books, 1979, 461.

12. Gormley, 299.

13. Kutler, Stanley I. *The Wars of Watergate*, New York: W.W. Norton, 1992, 391.

14. Kutler, 402.

15. Richardson, *Creative Balance*, 42, 38.

16. Richardson, in Gormley, xii.

17. Richardson, *Creative Balance*, 44; Gormley, 355.

18. Gormley, 355.

19. Gormley, 356; Richardson, *Creative Balance*, 44.

20. Richardson, *Creative Balance*, 44.

21. The American Presidency Project (www.presidency.ucsb.edu).

Richardson's letter of resignation went on to say: "In leaving your Administration, I take with me lasting gratitude for the opportunities you have given me to serve under your leadership in a number of important posts. It has been a privilege to share in your efforts to make the structure of world peace more stable and the structure of our own government more responsive. I believe profoundly in the rightness and importance of these efforts, and I trust that they will meet with increasing success in the remaining years of your presidency." President Nixon wrote back that same day, "It is with the deepest regret and with an understanding of the circumstances which brought you to your decision that I accept your resignation."

22. Bork's role in firing Cox impacted his unsuccessful nomination to the Supreme Court under President Reagan. See the YouTube video of Richardson speaking on behalf of Bork at Congressional hearings: www.youtube.com/watch2v=IM1cjDEIQxU

23. Richardson, Creative Balance, 45 and Gormley, 357.

24. Drew, Elizabeth. *Washington Journal: Reporting Watergate and Richardson Nixon's Downfall,* New York: Overlook Duckworth, 2014, 64.

25. Holzhausen, Richard L. Interview with Richardson, April 25, 1997, Gerald R. Ford Presidential Foundation Oral History Program, box 1, 7-8. See Appendix C.

26. Ruckelshaus, William. "Elliot Richardson's Choice," *The Washington Post,* January 5, 2000.

8: The Court of St. James

Chapter heading quotes:
- Robert Trowbridge Hartman, letter to the author, February 22, 1995.
- James P. Pfiffner, Elliot L. Richardson: Exemplar of Integrity and Public Service, *Public Integrity,* Vol. 5, No. 3 (Summer 2003), 267.

1. Miller, Norman C. "Elliot Richardson is a Man with a Past, Maybe a Big Future," *The Wall Street Journal,* February 22, 1974, 1.

2. Thompson, Kenneth W (editor). "The Paradox: Elliot L. Richardson," Vol. 6, *The Nixon Presidency* (Portraits of American Presidents series), University Press of America, 1987, 64;

Richardson, in Feinberg, 13.

3. *The Times* (London), "US-British Relations Were Never Better," March 12, 1975, 9; *The New Yorker*, Ambassador, November 10, 1975, 40, 42.

4. United Press International (wire story), "Richardson Counts Self Out for '76," June 17, 1975.

5. Gormley, 246, 248.

9: Returning to the Cabinet

Chapter heading quotes:
 - Former President Gerald R. Ford, letter to the author, April 7, 1994. See Appendix B.
- Richard Darman, in Spencer S. Hsu, "Washington Honors Elliot Richardson," *The Washington Post*, January 16, 2000.

1. Ford, Gerald R. *A Time to Heal*, New York: Harper & Row, 1979, 328.

2. *Congressional Record*, Senate Committee on Commerce (serial no. 94-57), 1976, 78-79.

3. *NOAA Magazine*, "A Message from the Secretary," April (No.6), 1976.

4. Cannon, James. *Time and Chance: Gerald Ford's Appointment with History*, New York: Harper Collins, 1994, 337, 402.

5. *Congressional Record*, Senate, Committee on Commerce (serial no. 94-57), 1976, 98.

6. Hess, Stephen. Review of "The Creative Balance," *The New York Times Book Review*, August 29, 1976. Also see George F. Will's column about *The Creative Balance*, "The Words of Elliot Richardson," *The Washington Post*, June 27, 1976.

7. Gerald R. Ford Presidential Library, Department of Commerce file, box 98 (folder file FG21), November 16, 1976.

10: Law of the Sea

Chapter heading quote:
- Vivek Viswanathan, *Crafting the Law of the Sea: Elliot Richardson and the Search for Order on the Oceans, (1977-1980)*, Harvard thesis, 2009, 125.

Commentary:
President Carter pushed for a speedy confirmation of Richardson for this post (Richardson being one of the few Republicans appointed to a highly visible post in his new administration). A White House memo dated February 18, 1977, mentions how the President wished to waive all checks on Richardson during this process, adding that "If the normal Senate nominating process" is not accomplished, "President Carter wants to appoint Mr. Richardson in such a way that does not require confirmation." On February 24, 1977, President Carter wrote to Senator Robert C. Byrd, "I really appreciate your assistance in expediting the confirmation of Elliot Richardson, Stansfield Turner and Warren Christopher."

1. Cyrus R. Vance interview (see Appendix A). For biographical information on Vance see the page one obituary "Cyrus R. Vance is Dead at 84; Statesman Served 3 Presidents" by Marilyn Berger, *The New York Times*, Jan. 13, 2002. The first paragraph of the obituary began with the fact that Vance, "who after two decades in public service was appointed secretary of state ... took the rare step of resigning from the nation's highest cabinet post on a matter of principle." He resigned in protest over President Carter's decision to launch a rescue of the American hostages held in Iran, an action "that he considered ill advised and futile," wrote Berger, and which failed (p. 1). The final paragraph of the full-page continuation from page one read: "Mr. Vance never dwelled on his own legacy, but when asked at 70 how he wanted to be remembered, he said, "I hope for being a reasonably decent, honest person who tried to do some things for the country that might have lasting effect and create a better life for a large number of people" (30).

2. Richardson, *Reflections*, 218.

3. Cyrus Vance interview.

4. Richardson, *Reflections*, 142.

5. Wertenbaker, William. "The Law of the Sea," *The New Yorker*,

Part 1, August 1, 1983, 39.

6. Mayer, Martin. *The Diplomats*, New York: Doubleday, 1983, 293.

7. Wertenbaker, Part 2, August 8, 64.

8. Richardson speech, Department of State, Current Policy Speech No. 60, March 1979.

9. Wertenbaker, Part 1, 45.

10. Richardson, *Reflections*, 217.

11. Wertenbaker, Part 1, 41, 40.

11: Legacy

Chapter heading quotes:
-Jonathan Moore, phone interview with the author, May 15, 2004.
-Richard Darman, introducing Richardson who was addressing a session of the Council for Excellence in Government's Whitehead Forum, reported in "Building Trust in Government: Elliot Richardson's Four 'Easy' Steps" in the Council's E-News, January/February, 1999.

Commentary:
- While visiting Harvard in 1998 as the speaker for Law Day, Richardson told the Harvard Crimson, chuckling, "I have sometimes referred to myself as occupying four of the world's most vilified professions – I was or am a politician, a bureaucrat, a lawyer and a diplomat" ("Richardson Stands Above 'Vilified" Legal World," by Stephanie K. Clifford, *The Harvard Crimson*, June 3, 1998).
- James Bennet, writing in the annual *The New York Times Magazine* section "The Lives They Lived" for 2001, ended his piece, "The Longest Day," with: "It is sad, really, that history honors Richardson more for quitting the government than for how hard he tried to keep working for it." (24).

1. Richardson. *Uses and Limitations of Law*, 35.

2. Richardson, *Uses and Limitations of Law*, 12-13.

3. Richardson, Elliot. "Civil Servants: Why Not the Best?" *The Wall Street Journal*, November 20, 1987, 28.

4. President George H.W. Bush, in Remarks at the Welcoming Ceremony for President Corazon C. Aquino of the Philippines, November 9, 1989, George Bush Presidential Library and Museum.

5. Drinan, Robert F. "Been There: Observations for the present from two politicians of the past," *New York Times Book Review* (also reviewing Gary Hart's *The Patriot*), July 28, 1996. Drinan also writes how Richardson "ponders throughout this thoughtful volume on the role of law" and says how some readers "will be disappointed that Mr. Richardson, detached almost to a fault, tells us almost nothing about his personal reactions or emotions." Finally, the reviewer comments that, "If a new generation of voters accepted the approach he proffers, they could transform the Republican Party and the nation."

6. *The New Yorker*, "Ambassador," 42.

7. Richardson, *Reflections*, 139, 205.

8. Gerald R. Ford letter (see Appendix B); Wyzomirski, Margaret J., "Elliot Richardson," *Political Profiles: The Nixon/Ford Years*, edited by Eleanora W. Schoenebaum, New York: Facts on File, 1979, 528.

9. Richardson, in Berman's *Courage of Convictions*, 205, 206-207.

10. Thompson, 51-52.

11. Reich, David, "Profile: Elliot Richardson – A Late Encounter with Mr. Clean," *World* (Unitarian Universalist) magazine, January/February 1997, 22.

BIBLIOGRAPHY

Presidential Libraries

Dwight D. Eisenhower Library

Richardson letter to former President Eisenhower, August 19, 1964, regarding Richardson's candidacy for Massachusetts lieutenant governor.

Nixon Presidential Library & Museum

Elliot L. Richardson, transcript of oral history interview by Frederick J. Graboske, May 31, 1988. Jonathan Moore, oral history interview, by Timothy J. Naftali, February 11, 2008. Both interviews are a part of the Nixon Project Oral Histories.

Gerald R. Ford Presidential Library and Museum

Richard L. Holzhausen, interview with ELR, April 25, 1997, Gerald R. Ford Foundation Oral History Program, box 1; A. James Reichley, interview with ELR, January 9, 1978, A. James Reichley Interview Transcripts 1977-1981, Domestic Policy: ELR, box 2; Richardson to President Ford, letter dated Nov. 16, 1976, Department of Commerce Subject File, box 98, folder file FG21.

Jimmy Carter Library

Diana Rock, Presidential Personnel Office to Rick Hutcheson, Feb. 18, 1977, regarding Richardson's nomination as ambassador for Law of the Sea negotiations; President Jimmy Carter to Senator Robert Byrd, Feb. 24, 1977, regarding confirmation of Richardson for ambassador for Law of the Sea negotiations; President Jimmy Carter to Richardson, Oct. 4, 1980, accepting Richardson's resignation as Ambassador for Law of the Sea negotiations.

Appointment of ELR as Special Representative of the President for the Multicultural Assistance Initiative for the Philippines, November 8, 1989; Remarks at the Welcoming Ceremony for President Corazon C. Aquino of the Philippines, November 9, 1989; Remarks to Members of the National Governors Association thanking Richardson, among others, for efforts assisting with the election in Nicaragua, February 26, 1990. Also, see the George H.W. Bush Oral History program, Interview with Carla Hills, January 6, 2004, Miller Center, University of Virginia, which includes the story about her joining the Department of Justice during the Watergate drama.

Selected Author Interviews and Correspondence

Gerald R. Ford, letter, April 7, 1994.

Elliot Richardson, personal interview in Washington, D.C., June 15, 1994.

Cyrus Vance (no relation), telephone interview, April 24, 1995.

Selected Works by Elliot Richardson

Books

The Creative Balance: Government, Politics, and the Individual in America's Third Century, New York: Holt Rinehard and Winston, 1976.

The Uses and Limitations of Law, New Delhi: Tata McGraw-Hill, 1982.

Reflections of a Radical Moderate, New York: Pantheon Books, 1996.

Speeches

"Aims and Strategy of U.S. Foreign Policy," before the American Political Science Association, New York City, September 5, 1969 (Department of State publication 8496, October 1969, reprinted in the *Congressional Record*, House, September 9, 1969, 24916).

"The United States and Western Europe," before the Chicago Council on Foreign Relations, Chicago, Illinois (*Congressional Record*, Senate, January 23, 1970, 921).

Address before the Second National Convocation on the Challenge of Building Peace, New York City, April 29, 1970 (*Congressional Record*, House, June 10, 1970, 19286).

"Toward a Workable Federalism," before the National Association of Counties Annual Meeting, Atlanta, Georgia, July 27, 1970 (booklet, Department of Health, Education and Welfare, US Government Printing Office, 1970).

The Agony of Watergate: Vulnerability and Vigilance," before the Appeal of Conscience Foundation Dinner, New York City, December 11, 1973 (*Representative American Speeches: 1973-1974*, edited by Waldo W. Braden, The Reference Shelf series, vol. 46, no. 3, New York: H.W. Wilson Company, 1974).

"The Case for Security Assistance to Other Nations," San Antonio, Texas, March 30, 1973 (*Congressional Record*, Extensions of Remarks, April 4, 1973, 11117).

"Restoring the Health of the Republican Party," before the Washington Press Club, 1974 (*Congressional Record*, Extensions of Remarks, December 14, 1974, 39970).

" Law of the Sea: A Test for the United Nations," before the Washington Press Club, March 14, 1979 (Department of State *Current Policy*, No. 60, March 1979).

"Amending the Constitution: Advice for the Future," before Constitution Day observances at the National Archives, Washington, D.C., September 17, 1997 (*The Washington Spectator*, November 15, 1977).

Contributions to books

Foreword to *The World of Roger Tory Peterson: An Authorized Biography*, by John C. Devlin and Grace Naismith, pp. xi-xiii, New York: Times Books, 1977.

Foreword, *Representing America: Experience of U.S. Diplomats at the United Nations*, by Linda M. Fasulo, New York: Facts-on-File, 1985.

"Elliot L. Richardson," in *The Courage of Convictions*, edited by Phillip L. Berman, pp. 201-207, New York: Ballantine, 1986.

Foreword, *Watergate: Scandal in the White House*, by Barbara Silberdick Feinberg, pp. 9-13, New York: Franklin Watts, 1990.

Foreword, *Archibald Cox: Conscience of a Nation*, by Ken Gormley, ix-xii, Reading, Massachusetts: Addison-Wesley, 1997.

Articles

"Freedom of Expression and the Function of Courts," *Harvard Law Review* 65, no. 1 (November 1951): 1-54.

"Poisoned Politics: The Real Tragedy of Massachusetts," *Atlantic Monthly*, October 1961, 77-81.

"A Personal Appreciation" (tribute to Felix Frankfurter), *Harvard Law School Bulletin* (March 1965).

"Taking the Global View," published in *The Washington Post*," reprinted in the *Congressional Record*, Senate, December 17, 1974, 40445.

"The Saturday Night Massacre," *Atlantic Monthly*, March 1976, 40-44, 69-71.

"The Sexless Orgies of Morality," *The New York Times Magazine*, January 23, 1977, 33.

"Nice, Wise, Astute: He Did Politics Honor" (on Everett Saltonstall), *Boston Globe*, June 18, 1979; reprinted in *Congressional Record* (Senate), June 18, 1979, 15201-15202.

"Power, Mobility and the Law of the Sea," *Foreign Affairs* 58, no. 4 (Spring 1980), 902-919.

" 'Fortress America' is Out of Date," *The Wall Street Journal*, July 10, 1980.

"Elliot Richardson on the Seabed Talks," *The Wall Street Journal*, March 9, 1981.

"The Rule in Cox's Case," *Harvard Law School Bulletin* (Fall 1982).

"Civil Servants: Why Not the Best?" *The Wall Street Journal*, November 20, 1987.

"Creating a Real Cabinet" (with James Pfiffner), *USA Today Magazine*, September 1990, pp. 10-12.

"A High-Tech Watergate," *The New York Times*, October 21, 1991.

"Let the Employer Provide" (with Arthur Flemming), *The Washington Post*, June 12, 1994.

"Treasure Beneath the Sea," *The New York Times*, July 30, 1994.

"Special Counsels, Petty Cases," *The New York Times*, June 5, 1995.

"Rara Avis: Roger Tory Peterson, Naturalist and Artist," *Yankee* 59, September 1995, 50.

Other Published Sources

Bar Report, "Legends in the Law: A Conversation with Elliot L. Richardson," District of Columbia Bar Association, February/March 1995.

Barnes, Bart. "Anne Richardson Dies; Literary Group Leader was Cabinet Spouse," *The Washington Post*, July 28, 1999.

Cannon, James. *Time and Chance: Gerald Ford's Appointment with History*, New York: Harper Collins, 1994.

Clifford, Stephanie. "Richardson Stands Above Vilified," *The Harvard Crimson*, June 3, 1998.

Cohen, Richard M., and Jules Witcover, *A Heartbeat Away: The Investigation and Resignation of Vice President Spiro T. Agnew*, New York: Viking Press, 1974.

Crewdson, John M. "Richardson Quits Over Order on Cox: Attorney General Says He Couldn't Oust Prosecutor, Cites Autonomy Vow," *The New York Times* (page one), October 21, 1973.

Current Biography, "Elliot Lee Richardson," Bronx, New York: H. W. Wilson, 1971, 343.

Drew, Elizabeth. *Washington Journal: Reporting Watergate and Richard Nixon's Downfall*, New York: Overlook Duckworth, 2014 (originally published as *Washington Journal: The Events of 1973-1974*, New York: Vintage Press, 1975).

Drury, Allen. *Courage and Hesitation: Notes and Photographs of the Nixon Administration* (photos by Fred Maroon), Doubleday, 1971.

Feeney, Mark. "Elliot Richardson, Versatile Man, Is Dead," *The Boston Globe*, January 1, 2000.

Ford, Gerald R., *A Time to Heal*, New York: Harper & Row, 1979.

Gormley, Kenneth. *Archibald Cox: Conscience of a Nation*, Reading, Massachusetts: Addison-Wesley, 1997.

Green, Wayne, "Mr. Clean: For Elliot Richardson, The Agnew Case May Be a Step to Presidency; Boston Liberal, Who Has Won Over Staff and Public, Said to Eye White House; 'Not Some Political Hack'," *The Wall Street Journal*, October 12, 1973, 1.

Haig, Alexander M., Jr. *Inner Circles*, New York: Warner Books, 1992.

Harriger, Katy J. *The Special Prosecutor in American Politics*, University Press of Kansas, 2000.

Hsu, Spencer, "Washington Honors Elliot Richardson: Admirers Commemorate 'A Great Public Servant,' *The Washington Post*, Jan. 16, 2000.

Kutler, Stanley I. *The Wars of Watergate*, New York: W.W. Norton, 1992.

Lewis, Neil. "Elliot Richardson Dies at 79; Stood Up to Nixon and Resigned in 'Saturday Night Massacre," *The New York Times*, January 1, 2000.

Lydon, Christopher, "The Choice for HEW: Elliot Lee Richardson," *New York Times*, June 8, 1970. Reprinted in *The New York Times Biographical Edition*, vol. 1, April/June 1990.

------, "Richardson and Justice," *The New York Times*, May 20, 1973. Reprinted in *The New York Times Biographical Edition*, May 1973.

------, "Richardson 'Cousins' Fill a Hall," *The Boston Globe*, January 19, 1967 (page 1 of the morning edition) .

McCloud, Bill. *What Should We Tell Our Children About Vietnam?*, Norman: University of Oklahoma Press, 1989.

Miller, Norman C., "Elliot Richardson is a Man with a Past, Maybe a Big Future," *The Wall Street Journal*, February 22, 1974, 1.

Nyhan, David. "Elliot Richardson: A Winner Where It Truly Counted," *The Boston Globe*, January 16, 2000.

National Journal, "Elliot Richardson's Tenure as HEW Secretary: Many Defeats and Frustrations, Taken in Spirit of Loyalty," vol. 5, no. 1, January 6, 1973.

NBC *Meet the Press*, Guest Elliot Richardson, The Secretary of Defense, April 1, 1973.

NBC *Meet the Press*, Guest: Elliot Richardson, April 28, 1974.

NBC *Meet the Press*, Guest: Elliot Richardson, The Secretary of Commerce, August 8, 1976.

Newsweek, "Richardson: Nixon's Brahmin," December 11, 1972.

Nixon, Richard. *The Memoirs of Richard Nixon*, New York: Warner Books, 1979.

Palmer, Bruce, Jr. *The Twenty-Five-Year War: America's Military Role in Vietnam*, Lexington: University Press of Kentucky, 1984.

Reich, David, "Profile: Elliot Richardson – A Late Encounter with Mr. Clean," *World* (Unitarian Universalist) magazine, January/February 1997.

Reston, James, "Wrong-Way Richardson," *The New York Times*, February 28, 1975, 33.

Royster, Vermont. "Thinking Things Over," *The Wall Street Journal*, February 11, 1976.

Ruckelshaus, William D. "Elliot Richardson's Choice," *The Washington Post*, January 5, 2000.

Shawcross, William. "Virtue Rewarded," Sunday Times Magazine (London), March 23, 1975.

Silberdick-Feinberg, Barbara. *Watergate: Scandal in the White House*, Twentieth Century American History series, New York: Franklin Watts, 1990.

Szulc, Tad, "The Smile on the Face of Elliot Richardson," *Esquire*, July, 1974.

Time, "The Presidential Cleanup Crew," May 14, 1973.

Time, 'Richard Nixon Stumbles to the Brink," October 29, 1973. Includes a side-bar article, "The Three Men of High Principle," consisting of "Short profiles of the three men who stood on principle, defied the President and lost their jobs."

The New Yorker, "Ambassador," November 10, 1975.

Thompson, Kenneth, W., editor, "The Paradox: Elliot L. Richardson," *Portraits of American Presidents* series, vol. 6, *The Nixon Presidency*, 51-70, University Press of America, 1987.

Vivek Viswanathan, *Crafting the Law of the Sea: Elliot Richardson and the Search for Order on the Oceans, (1977-1980)*, Harvard thesis, 2009.

Wertenbacker, William, "The Law of the Sea," *The New Yorker*, August 1 and August 8, 1983.

White, Theodore. *Breach of Faith*, New York: Reader's Digest Press, 1975.

Wyzomirski, Margaret J., "Elliot Richardson," *Political Profiles: The Nixon/Ford Years*, editor, Eleanora W. Schoenebaum, New York: Facts on File, 1979, 524-528.

ACKNOWLEDGMENTS

My thanks to Nicholas V. Prass for bringing the voice of a new generation to this story in our Foreword and for proofing this edition ...

Tom Coyne, Vice President Emeritus, Western Michigan University, for his counsel during the preparation of both editions ...

Author Dave Dempsey who helped with both editions, and Judge Derwin Rushing for his assistance with drafts of the original edition – both early supporters of my initial research ...

Ken Gormley, J.D., for his guidance with the initial manuscript and for his helpful scholarship on Richardson found in his biography of Archie Cox ...

My brother Dave, friends Dr. John and Debbie Sinclair, Daryl Longman, and biographer Linda H. Davis, and the many colleagues at The Upjohn Company – and later Pharmacia & Upjohn – for their encouragement ...

Dr. Bradley Hayden for an inspiring classroom setting for the idea ...

The late Donald Carr, J.D., and the late Robert McDonough, J.D., for their encouragement and assistance throughout the years ...

And to my wife Kathy and daughter Kelly who patiently accompanied me on my six-year journey during the 1990s to tell this story of one of our nation's greatest public servants – and to Kathy and Kelly again, and son-in-law Rob, for being a ready audience for my continued fascination with Richardson's career.

For the original edition

This work was made possible, in part, by a travel grant from the Gerald R. Ford Presidential Foundation. Many thanks to family and friends for their advice; to the Council for Excellence in Government, especially Patricia McGinnis and Sean D'Souza; and to editor Madeline Adams.

Visit the author on LinkedIn
www.linkedin.com/pub/tom-vance/59/982/248/

TOPICAL INDEX

Made in the USA
Charleston, SC
02 October 2014